Domestic Violence Matters: an evaluation of a development project

Liz Kelly

with
Julie Bindel, Sheila Burton, Dianne Butterworth,
Kate Cook and Linda Regan
Child and Woman Abuse Studies Unit
University of North London.

**A Research Development and
Statistics Directorate Report**

London: Home Office

Home Office Research Studies

The Home Office Research Studies are reports on research undertaken by or on behalf of the Home Office. They cover the range of subjects for which the Home Secretary has responsibility. Titles in the series are listed at the back of this report (copies are available from the address on the back cover). Other publications produced by the Research, Development and Statistics Directorate include Research Findings, the Research Bulletin, Statistical Bulletins and Statistical Papers.

The Research, Development and Statistics Directorate

The Research, Development and Statistics Directorate is an integral part of the Home Office, serving the Ministers and the department itself, its services, Parliament and the public through research, development and statistics. Information and knowledge from these sources informs policy development and the management of programmes; their dissemination improves wider public understanding of matters of Home Office concern.

First published 1999

Application for reproduction should be made to the Information and Publications Group, Room 201, Home Office, 50 Queen Anne's Gate, London SW1H 9AT.

©Crown copyright 1999 ISBN 1 84082 137 X
ISSN 0072 6435

Foreword

The remit of the Programme Development Unit, set up in 1992 within what is now the Research Development and Statistics Directorate, is to encourage, fund and evaluate innovative local approaches to problems of crime and criminality and to disseminate messages emerging for policy and practice. One aim is to bridge the gap between research and policy by testing out practical developments, to see what does and doesn't work. The emphasis in the project evaluations is not on 'success' or 'failure' but on learning from experience. The focus is on how and why interventions are or are not effective and the evaluations look closely at process as well as outcomes.

In the initial phase of the PDU programme, project work focused on two themes: domestic violence and early intervention with children and young people. The second phase, which began in 1996, is carrying forward the early intervention theme.

This report documents the evaluation of Domestic Violence Matters, an experimental project in Islington, London, based loosely on a scheme in London, Ontario. Domestic Violence Matters located civilian crisis counsellors in two police stations in Islington, operating an out of office hours service. The aims were not only to provide much needed support to victims at their most vulnerable point but also to enhance the response of the criminal justice system to the crime of domestic violence and to secure better informed and co-ordinated responses by local agencies to the problem.

Domestic violence is an important public policy issue. Over the last 25 years, various initiatives have been launched, from refuges through legislative and institutional changes to inter-agency groups and work with violent men. Despite these developments, domestic violence remains a serious and deeply damaging problem for which effective responses are not yet in place. In particular, as the evaluation of this project shows, there is still some way to go in establishing the firm principle that domestic violence is as much a crime as any other.

The project achieved a great deal and this report makes a significant contribution to our knowledge and understanding in this area.

If you would like to know more about the work of the Programme Development Unit, please contact Room 820, Home Office, Queen Anne's Gate, London SW1H 9AT, Tel. 0171 273 2902 Fax. 0171 273 3674.

C P NUTTALL

Acknowledgements

I should like to express my appreciation to the many people whose co-operation was essential to conducting this evaluation. Firstly, to the Metropolitan Police Service and particularly to those officers in Holloway and Islington divisions who participated in the experimental project and its evaluation. Particular thanks need to be given to Derek Talbot and Paul Mathias whose commitment to both Domestic Violence Matters and its evaluation was invaluable. The support of the Management Group was essential and to each of them I give my thanks. Without the participation and understanding of the staff of Domestic Violence Matters, the evaluation could not have proceeded. I am grateful to Christine Lehman and Lorna Smith of the Home Office Programme Development Unit for their constructive criticism throughout the writing of this report. Finally, my especial gratitude to the many women who were helped by the project and who chose to be part of the evaluation process.

Dr. Liz Kelly

Contents

Glossary

DVM:	Domestic Violence Matters
DVU:	Domestic Violence Unit
HOPDU/PDU:	Home Office Programme Development Unit
EG:	Executive Group
PMG:	Programme Management Group
MC:	Management Committee
NI:	New Islington Division
NH:	Holloway Division
LADVC:	Local Authority Domestic Violence Co-ordinator
IVSS:	Islington Victim Support Service
CPS:	Crown Prosecution Service

Executive summary

Domestic violence matters

Domestic Violence Matters (DVM) is an adaption of a Canadian project – the Family Consultancy Service (London, Ontario) and involves locating a team of skilled civilian crisis interveners within the police service to follow up police responses to domestic violence.

The joint sponsors of DVM were the Metropolitan Police and the Islington Safer Cities Project; the pilot was to cover both Islington and Holloway police divisions.

The key aims of the pilot were: establishing civilian crisis intervention; promoting a law enforcement response; and developing inter-agency links to encourage consistent and co-ordinated responses.

The project staff comprised a co-ordinator, four 'support workers' and an administrator; managed by a small management committee and larger advisory group.

Crisis intervention was available 16 hours a day (10am – 2am), seven days a week, fifty-two weeks a year. DVM was to be called in the event of arrest, in the hope that support would increase the woman's ability and willingness to pursue prosecution, and was to be offered to all other victims.

The evaluation – structure and methods

The evaluation used a three phase multi-methodological strategy, including: participant observation; in-depth interviewing; project database creation and maintenance; and questionnaires. Police officers, service users and local agencies were surveyed. An action research model was also used, in order that findings could inform subsequent development.

Making a difference – crisis intervention

A crisis is 'any point at which routine coping strategies break down and the need or potential for change is present'.

Change was defined as increasing the emotional, social and material resources of victims.

An emphasis was placed on how coping strategies develop, can be barriers to seeking help, and are often mis-understood by professionals.

DVM provided crisis intervention responses to 1,236 individuals, in relation to 1,542 incidents.

A response within 24 hours was achieved in 90 per cent of cases.

Ninety-nine per cent of victims were female and 99 per cent of perpetrators male; 21 per cent of the women DVM worked with were Black and a further 10 per cent from ethnic minorities; 5 per cent were disabled.

Over two-thirds of referrals were received outside normal office hours.

DVM was successful in reducing repeat calls from the same individual.

The workers and women users stressed that early pro-active intervention is effective in enabling change; users attributed their ability to end relationships and/or proceed with legal action to DVM.

Crisis intervention extends beyond the incident and includes short-term support and advocacy, and in some instances longer term contact.

A phased model of coping with domestic violence and appropriate crisis interventions has been developed.

Policing and law enforcement

Police record keeping at all levels, in relation to domestic violence, is neither systematic nor consistent.

Various measures of arrests rates before and during the course of the pilot produced equivocal results; whatever impact DVM had was limited.

Even where an offence is recorded by police, arrest and/or charges occur in a minority of incidents.

In a third or more of cases the perpetrator is not present when police arrive, and there is minimal follow up in these circumstances.

Both a section of the police and some prosecutors work from a presumption that women will withdraw; this becomes a self fulfilling prophecy.

Support for law enforcement approaches is fragile; factors influencing whether or not police arrest are frequently not matters of law but value judgements about 'victim worthiness' and on the spot assessments about likelihood of withdrawal, that the incident is a 'one off', and previous calls to the same address.

Neither divisional nor force policy have become routine aspects of daily practice.

DVM increased confidence in the police amongst victims, and decreased repeat calls; there is a suggestion that in one division this resulted in a significant decrease in overall calls to the police.

Police, courts and prosecutors fail to ensure that victim witnesses are provided with the protection necessary to enable them to give evidence.

Where women are enabled to pursue prosecution conviction is likely, most commonly through a guilty plea.

Women want respectful treatment by, and assertive action from the police – but they do not always receive either or both.

Victims of domestic violence think domestic violence should be responded to as a crime, but need support and protection in order for this to be a viable option.

Inter-agency links and co-ordination

At the outset relatively low levels of awareness were found in both the statutory and voluntary sector.

The voluntary sector is used more frequently than the statutory sector in help seeking.

The development of complementary working with the Local Authority Domestic Violence Co-ordinator resulted in several initiatives to address gaps in provision, and linked action in relation to poor practice.

Over the duration of the pilot, knowledge of local resources developed enabling more appropriate referrals and advocacy.

Most of DVM's users were not aware of the extent of support they could access, and significant numbers followed through referrals to other agencies.

DVM became a valued local resource amongst a number of agencies; two-thirds of the agencies DVM worked most closely with thought it had changed their practice, making them both more informed and sensitive to the varied needs of women.

It was the DVM workers daily practice of crisis intervention, acting as advocates for individual women with other agencies, which proved most effective in developing consistent and co-ordinated responses.

DVM's importance locally was attributed to availability out of hours, their role as advocates for women, and the linking and co-ordination role they performed.

The DVM pilot offers a model of how to create local catalysts for change, through 'case advocacy', for both individuals suffering domestic violence and agency practice, although senior level impetus for change was not as effective as originally envisaged.

Telling the story - process evaluation

DVM went 'live' in February 1993 and the pilot involved a total of 32 months direct service.

Quality crisis intervention was provided throughout the pilot.

Working across two police divisions created substantial problems, making the achievement of common practice and effective monitoring of police responses virtually impossible.

Police referrals varied between the two divisions and over time, dropping significantly in the final year.

The initial hostility and wariness to DVM of police officers was converted by the end of the pilot to respectful co-operation.

Strong working links were built with many other local agencies especially through the work of crisis intervention, and some initial sceptics and critics became strong supporters.

Management of the project was unwieldy, and because of this at times less effective than it might have been.

Power and position frequently became barriers to progress – both through its use as a veto, and failure to use it.

Reflections, conclusions and recommendations

The DVM model of crisis intervention is effective, although not in the same ways for each individual; the closer the intervention was to the model outline – personalised immediate contact soon after an incident – the more difference it made.

Despite the under-utilisation, DVM worked intensively with as many, if not more women than other specialist domestic violence services.

Pro-active projects which seek to engage women and keep in touch in order to accelerate change processes offer considerable scope for enhancing local domestic violence provision.

Substantial institutional barriers exist in the police which are hampering implementation of policy; these need to be addressed as a matter of urgency.

The current legislative and policy context along with (lack of) enforcement practices represent fundamental stumbling blocks to implementing the principle that domestic violence is a crime. Without substantial changes any movement in this direction will be minimal and not integrated across the criminal justice system.

1 Introduction – Domestic Violence Matters

Over the last quarter of a century the prevalence of domestic violence[1] and its physical and emotional consequences for women and their children has been documented in many countries (Dobash and Dobash, 1992; Heise, 1994). International recognition is evident in research, innovative legal reform, support and advocacy projects and public and professional education programmes. Governments were asked to commit themselves to decreasing the prevalence of domestic violence (and all forms of violence against women) in the UN Platform for Action agreed at the Beijing conference in 1995.

It was feminists, last century (see Gordon 1988, Pleck, 1987) and this, who both named the violence women experienced at the hands of male partners[2] and pointed to the failure of governments, legal systems and social agencies to recognise it, let alone respond appropriately and effectively. New forms of provision emerged through localised women's activism: refuges, safe houses and helplines now exist on every continent. Campaigns for reform have produced new legislation, policies for law enforcement, policy and practice guidelines covering health, housing and social welfare, and education programmes aimed at young people, offenders, professionals and the general public (Dobash and Dobash, 1992; Edelman and Eisocovits, 1996).

Underlying all of these responses and reforms is an understanding that the abuse women suffer is deliberate, persistent and frequently life threatening, and involves actions which in most countries constitute criminal assault. Failure to respond because the interactions occur in the 'private' sphere, within 'intimate' relationships, denies women a fundamental aspect of citizenship – the right to personal safety and protection under the law – and allows violence to continue unchecked. It is a measure of the success of women's organisations that other agencies, organisations and governments, in some countries, have committed themselves to responding to domestic violence as a crime.

---

1 The term 'domestic violence' is used throughout this report, partly because it is the focus (and name) of the project being evaluated, and it is a term used by many other agencies, including the police. As a concept, however, it fails to accurately name and locate the issue.

2 Whilst a small proportion of domestic violence cases involve a woman using violence against a man, or lesbian and gay relationships, throughout this report women will be referred to as the victims and men as the perpetrators of violence. Data from this study, police records from Greater Manchester (GMP, 1994, 1995) and countless research projects (Dobash and Dobash, 1992) confirm that the distribution of victimisation and offending is gendered.

The Islington pilot project – Domestic Violence Matters (DVM) – is one example in British exploration of changing responses to domestic violence. It builds on recent changes in policing policy (see Grace, 1995), seeking to augment this through the provision of civilian follow up crisis intervention.

The basic idea behind DVM is drawn from Canada (originally based in, and sometimes referred to as the 'London, Ontario' model) and involves locating a team of skilled civilian crisis interveners within the police service. The Family Consultant Service (FCS) was introduced as a two-year pilot in London, Ontario in 1972. It reflected current thinking about the role mediation could play in policing practice. The basic framework was that three civilian 'consultants' would provide front line assistance to police intervention in 'family disputes'. FCS was *never* confined to domestic violence,[3] although the published evaluations have all focused on this aspect, and its reputation largely rests on what has never been more than a quarter of the project's work.

Police would attend callouts, do what was necessary and within their powers, and where appropriate call out the 'consultants'. Their role was to assess the situation, provide some immediate crisis counselling, arrange for any necessary follow-up and make referrals to other agencies. What made the service unique was that the workers were available on call, seven days a week and the close link with the police. The 'consultants' were also to be a bridge between the police and other agencies in the community, both in terms of active liaison and later through involvement in inter-agency forums. It was hoped that these working relationships and the possibilities for formal and informal networking would enhance the forms and content of available support in the local community. FCS has supported the development of a wide range of specialist domestic violence services, and is an active member of what is now called The London Co-ordinating Committee to End Woman Abuse.

The philosophy underpinning FCS is a version of crisis theory:

- in an emergency usual coping strategies are strained, this produces situations which are both high risk and opportunities for change;

- people's ability to cope depends on the extent to which they have access to appropriate resources and support;

- the stress of crises make people more open to/needy of help from the outside;

- an immediate intervention increases the likelihood that referrals to other agencies will be taken up.

---

3   FCS responds to all family issues which police are involved in; child abuse, disputes between parents and children, domestic violence, juvenile crime, mental health, homelessness and a variety of other issues.

By 1979 the staffing of FCS had increased to four workers and a co-ordinator. During the 1980s policing of domestic violence in Canada shifted to a more active law enforcement approach. Police in London had made very few arrests throughout the 1970s, although it was the first city in Ontario to adopt a pro-arrest stance following a 1982 policy directive from the Solicitor General. Prior to this only 3 per cent of calls resulted in arrest, although 20 per cent of victims required medical treatment, and there were "reasonable and probable grounds" for arrest in many more cases.

The current policy in Ontario is one of mandatory *charge* rather than mandatory arrest. Canada does not have federal legislation permitting 'presumptive' arrest and provinces cannot enact criminal law, thus precluding localised mandatory arrest policies (as have developed in areas of the US). A mandatory charge need not involve an arrest, what is required is that a charge is made formally. Charges are issued at the scene (or subsequently) and these take the form of an "appearance notice" (similar to a summons) specifying a date for court appearance. Formal arrangements exist whereby Crown Prosecutors keep police aware of the earliest court dates available, and officers at the scene call through to the station and are given the earliest possible court appearance date (usually within 7–10 days). Police are expected to lay the charges, not on the basis of the victims wishes, but the behaviour which prompted the call. In London, as in many other areas where police have taken on this responsibility, this resulted in a marked decrease in cases being dismissed/withdrawn. This has been further re-enforced by changed policies and practices for Crown Attorneys (the equivalent of the CPS) which include: that they see the victim within three weeks of the charge; a 'no-drop' policy for domestic violence offences; and dedicated domestic violence prosecutors.

The distinction between mandatory arrest and mandatory charge has not informed debate in Britain to date, where most discussion has focused on arrest policies. The police have drawn attention to the fact that many incidents of domestic violence do not include behaviour which is currently recognised as an 'arrestable offence', thus placing limits on what it is possible for them to do. Mandatory charge would sidestep these problems, and has the added advantage of the police taking pro-active responsibility for law enforcement. Speedy processing of cases also means that the long delays before cases are heard could be avoided. For such a policy to be effective the kinds of agreements evident in Canada between the police, prosecutors and courts would have to be instituted.[4] Canadian women's organisations have expressed reservations about the policy, since it discourages arrest which offers women a limited period of safety in which to make decisions.

---

4   There are potential tensions between mandatory charge and the police and CPS agreed 'case disposal' system (see Chapter Six). The introduction of trained special/dedicated prosecutors would have to be considered, as would fast tracking of cases, or even domestic violence courts which have begun the to emerge in the US and Canada.

Clearly the role of FCS in relation to domestic violence will have changed during the 1980s, but there is little written documentation of this.[5] Two studies of changing law enforcement policy (Jaffee et al. 1986, 1991) also included FCS; the former finding that the involvement of FCS in domestic violence cases enhanced positive outcomes and the latter that FCS increased access to specialist women's services.

This shift in law enforcement policy was accompanied in Ontario by a well resourced government initiative covering prosecution, prevention, support services and research. For example, The Women's Directorate spent half a million dollars training 52 Crown Attorneys in order that each district had a skilled domestic violence prosecutor. Other aspects of the pro-prosecution initiative included: all victims being interviewed by prosecutors within three weeks of a charge; a 'no drop' policy; an enhanced range of sentencing options; victim/witness advocacy programmes located in the prosecutor's office; emergency legal aid with an automatic right to one hour of free advice. As, if not more, were important provisions for: secure funding support for refuges;[6] recognition of women's need for safe temporary and permanent housing; education and training opportunities provided by refuges; a mass public education programme headed by the Women's Directorate, to include a prevention month and programmes in schools;[7] the development of 'multi-cultural' practice, including interpreting services and specific services for indigenous peoples.

Awareness of the London, Ontario model was relatively widespread amongst British police and domestic violence 'experts'; although two visits to Canada (one before DVM started and one half way through) revealed that what was 'known' was not particularly accurate. The possibility of a pilot in Britain was raised in the late 1980s, and one of the strongest advocates was a woman police officer based in Islington. In the early 1990s these discussions expanded to include the Islington Safer Cities Project.

A steering group was formally established on 15th November 1991 combining senior police officers from both Holloway and Islington divisions and the Islington Safer Cities Project. Their brief was to explore the viability of a pilot and if appropriate find funding for the project. The initial vision of DVM was that it would be based in one of the Islington police divisions. At the planning stage this was not acceptable to either the other division or Safer Cities. DVM was envisioned as working across two police divisions. The logistical and practical problems this created are addressed in more detail in Chapter Six. The Home Office Programme Development Unit (PDU)

---

5   Peter Jaffee, with colleagues, published an early evaluation of FCS and more recently a number of reports and papers on the impact of changing police responses to domestic violence in London, Ontario (see Jaffee et al. 1979, 1984, 1986, 1991, 1993). The 1986 study is attributed a central role in the development of national policies to encourage arrest and charge.

6   Called 'shelters' in Canada.

7   The 'Zero Tolerance' campaign developed by Edinburgh Women's Unit, and now adopted across Scotland and by many local authorities in England, drew inspiration from some of these developments.

aimed at developing innovative models in "preventing and reducing criminality and family violence" presented the funding opportunity. The pilot was selected as one of the three-year funded PDU projects in April 1992.

The commitment of the Metropolitan Police in initiating DVM, and in allowing virtually unprecedented access to both the DVM staff and the evaluator should be acknowledged at this early point. The routine daily contact that DVM had with DVUs, police officers and police records alongside the research elements of the evaluation meant that police practice was the subject of intense scrutiny. It was inevitable that shortcomings would be discovered in this process, and it is entirely to the credit of the police that access was never restricted.

Domestic Violence Matters

This section presents a brief description of DVM, its aims and objectives, the basic policy framework, what the work of the project comprised, and the original management structure. This description is augmented by the process evaluation in Chapter Six.

DVM sought to combine a pro-law enforcement stance towards domestic violence with the provision of crisis intervention. Whilst never intended as a 'replication' of FCS, it drew heavily on the model for inspiration. A core principle was that police responses to domestic violence were based on an "overriding priority, the protection of the victim and the apprehension of the offender" (Home Office Circular 60/1990).

The key aims of the pilot were:

- to use civilian support workers to assist the police with crisis intervention;

- to develop the fundamental principle in Islington that domestic violence is a crime and is dealt with accordingly; to this end the project workers will encourage action to be taken against the perpetrators and help ensure the protection of victims whilst addressing their ongoing needs;

- to contact all victims within 24 hours of a call being made to the police;

- by taking immediate action it is hoped that there will be a decrease in repeat calls and an increase in the likelihood of referrals to other agencies being taken up;

- to develop strong links with statutory and voluntary agencies, facilitate improved communication and increase the immediate and effective response of all agencies in the borough to domestic violence.

Islington is an inner London borough, with a mix of housing provision, relative wealth and relative deprivation. There has been a refuge in the borough since the 1970s, but limited additional work on domestic violence occurred in the borough in the 1980s. As part of the Islington Safer Cities Project commitment a post of 'Domestic Violence Co-ordinator' (LADVC), linked to the local authority Women's Unit, was funded to dovetail with DVM, although the appointment was made some months before DVM began. The post holder has been the catalyst for a number of initiatives and projects in the borough, including inter-agency good practice guidelines and training and an inter-agency forum.

Despite this, however, the local and national context in which DVM developed entailed few of the strong institutional, legislative supports and range of resources which have been present in London, Ontario for the last decade. Furthermore, changes in policing policy and practice in relation to domestic violence are still relatively recent in Britain, and have the status of guidelines rather than a coherent and formalised statutory policy encompassing all elements of the criminal justice system.

The basic structure of the project was that five civilian workers work alongside the police to enhance responses to domestic violence. The project staff comprised a co-ordinator, four 'support workers'[8] who delivered the direct service,[9] and for most of the pilot an administrator. A two-tier management structure was planned with a small Management Committee (MC) comprising a limited and specified membership who had positions to influence policy within their own organisations and a Project Advisory Group (PAG) with a broader membership, which was to act as a policy and practice forum.

The contribution of the Metropolitan Police to the project involved providing office space, a proportion of office supplies and an unmarked car. The car was to enable the support workers to attend call-outs speedily, and it was based at the station where the DVM office was established.

---

8   There were occasions when the co-ordinator and administrator undertook support work, to cover for sickness, holidays etc.

9   A further 24 line has recently been established by Northern Ireland Women's Aid, and in the last round of Lottery awards Refuge (based in London) received funding for an additional 24 hour service.

What distinguishes the DVM model is that it takes account of when domestic violence most commonly occurs – evenings and weekends. Only the 'emergency services' provide 24-hour cover, and in 1992 there was a single 24-hour domestic violence crisis line in Britain run by the Women's Aid Federation, England in Bristol.[10] Follow-up support – if there is any – usually takes place after the immediate crisis has passed. Police Domestic Violence Units (DVUs) echo this delayed response, with cases being picked up the morning after (at the earliest), and letters sent asking if victims[11] require any support or advice. A common misunderstanding regarding DVUs is that they respond to domestic violence calls; in some variants officers do investigative work, monitor and develop local police practice, but the majority are confined to collecting and collating local cases and providing various forms of 'victim support' (see also Glass 1995; Grace 1995; Walker and McNicol 1994).

What DVM sought to offer was immediate support and advice – crisis intervention. A shift system meant that support workers were available 16 hours a day (10am – 2am), seven days a week, fifty-two weeks a year.[12] This simple (albeit resource intensive) fact mattered a great deal to the users of DVM, many of whom made explicit comments about the importance of the support workers' availability (see Chapter Three).

The agreed protocol between DVM and the police was that DVM should be called out/offered immediately to every woman where an arrest occurred, in the hope that support would increase the woman's ability and willingness to pursue prosecution. In these circumstances the support worker would go out to the woman, or see her at the police station. DVM support would also be offered to all victims, but where the perpetrator was still in the household, or likely to return this would be done over the telephone, by bringing the woman to the police station or making an appointment as soon as possible. The precautions where an arrest had not taken place were necessary to ensure the safety of the support workers. When workers were on duty they could be reached by telephone or pager, and when attending a crisis call out they used the project car and took a mobile phone with them. Crisis intervention encompassed far more than supporting prosecution, and had at its heart the aim of enabling women to explore options in order to increase their own safety, and that of any children they had.

A programme of briefings to police officers in Islington began in early 1993 comprising an introduction to the project workers and the protocol

---

10   Whilst the use of the word 'victim' has been rejected by many women's organisations, this challenge relates to the stigmatising identity that accompanied its use. The word does, however, refer to the fact that someone has been victimised, and in the context of police and crisis intervention responses the immediacy of a recent assault is extremely salient. It is, therefore, used at times in this report to refer to individuals in the context of a recent assault or their position within legal processes (for further discussion see Kelly, Burton and Regan, 1996).

11   A 24 hour service would have required a team of five support workers; this was in the original tender, but funding was only forthcoming for four.

12   In interviews and discussions the support workers discussed the complexity of belief, that it does not necessarily mean taking every element of a woman's story at face value

between DVM and the police. A laminated pocket sized 'code memoire' was distributed to each officer which listed their powers and the procedure for calling out DVM. Supplies of local agency referral cards, in a similar format, were also provided which could be left with women. Re-briefings took place at regular intervals throughout the project.

Islington has two police divisions (referred to throughout this report as NI and NH) with separate command structures. Each division had a DVU, and both Chief Superintendents were part of the steering group and the management committee in the early stages of the project. DVM's office base was in the recently built NI station.

The theory of crisis intervention outlined above has informed the work of DVM throughout and is discussed in more detail in Chapter Three. There are, however, some additional basic principles which DVM rapidly developed and worked from throughout the project: that domestic violence encompasses physical, sexual, financial and emotional abuse; to believe women;[13] to name violence even if women were not doing so themselves; to communicate explicitly that abuse was not her fault, and that abusive men choose to use violence; that she deserved something better than this; that she had rights and options; that it was her choice what action to take.

The support offered to any particular woman varied considerably in terms of the location it took place in and its content. The location included emergency call outs to women's homes, meeting at the police station or another agreed neutral place, and telephone calls. Each of these could comprise basic advice, or answering a specific query through to lengthy conversations which encompassed the history of the relationship, women's confusions about this, the impacts of violence on them and the options which were open to them. The follow-up also varied from minimal to extensive. The latter was most common where women were: pursuing prosecution; requiring safe accommodation; having complicated legal matters with regard to property, custody and/or immigration status; being pursued by a determined abuser. Some women made only one contact, others many, over the pilot's life.

Whilst enhancing women's safety was the primary aim of crisis intervention, the support workers became increasingly adept at assessing the varying needs of women; for some it may be naming violence, for others having space to re-assess their relationship, still others wanted practical advice and information and some assistance in leaving violent men (see Chapter Three for a more detailed discussion).

---

13   At the time of writing DVM continues, albeit with a much smaller staff team, and is still seeking secure longer term funding.

What a 'case' subsequently involved also varied considerably depending on the decisions made by women as a consequence of the initial intervention. The DVM workers, rightly, saw it as their responsibility to do some form of follow up, and this again varied between a telephone call the next day, or several days later, through to acting as a temporary advocate to ensure that the options which women wanted to take up to increase their safety were feasible. For example, if a woman viewed her most viable option as a housing transfer, a letter from DVM supporting this request was likely to facilitate this sooner than the woman acting on her own behalf. Follow up advocacy is a vital component of crisis intervention, yet is different from the conventional longer term 'case work' model.

Where crisis intervention enables someone to take potentially major life decisions with far reaching consequences, there is a short term responsibility to ensure that the possibilities of maintaining that change are maximised. In the case of DVM this is a relatively time limited commitment to provide support which facilitates the pursuit of safety and an ending of violence. At its most mundane level the simple fact that support workers made follow up calls and were contactable outside office hours was a significant factor for a number of women, providing support to take, and hold to, hard decisions – especially proceeding with prosecution, applications for injunctions and/or leaving a violent partner.

Each DVM case was entered onto a database designed for the project, and a set of case notes developed. The case notes were essential as a record of previous actions, since the workers did not carry 'case loads'; the shift system and crisis intervention framework meant that whoever was on duty had to pick up outstanding work and respond to calls from police and users in that period. This aspect of DVM's structure appears to have worked well – with office systems ensuring that shift handovers noted urgent tasks and few service users complained about not having a designated person to deal with.

In terms of evaluation, there are three core elements to DVM: civilian crisis intervention following police intervention; promoting a law enforcement response; and developing inter-agency links to encourage consistent and co-ordinated responses. Chapters Three to Five address each of these themes separately whilst recognising that in reality they interacted in multiple and complex ways. Chapter Two outlines the structure of, and methods used in, the evaluation and Chapter Six is the process evaluation – telling 'the story' of DVM for the three years it was funded by PDU.[14]

---

14   Julie Bindel did this data collection and wrote a short report on record keeping which was discussed at a meeting between DVM and both DVUs.

2 The evaluation – structure and methods

The evaluation design comprised an element of the original project tender. It was conceived as a multi-methodological strategy, including participant observation, in-depth interviewing, database creation and maintenance and questionnaires. There were three phases, with police officers and local agencies receiving questionnaires and interviews with key players being conducted at designated intervals; at the start, mid and end points of the pilot. Keeping records of all DVM cases and sending evaluation questionnaires to users were ongoing throughout the three-year period. An integral element of the evaluation was an action research component, whereby regular feedback was given to the project in order that this could inform subsequent development. Several of the evaluation components were designed to have dual purposes, providing a resource for DVM, police DVUs and the LADVC as well as evaluative data. Much of the design work involved consultation with others.

Regular evaluation reports, both written and oral were given to the project, including an initial report in October 1992 on the barriers to increasing law enforcement responses and two interim reports in 1993 and 1994. Several additional elements were added to the evaluation (a questionnaire for women withdrawing their complaint; logs for DVUs; a follow up of cases through the prosecution process; evaluation of police training sessions; and two focus groups with police officers), and slight alterations to methodology were made where appropriate (the third phase agency survey was done by telephone to increase response rates).

The work undertaken, and data collected, for the evaluation of DVM is listed below.

- Compiling baseline comparison data from six months of police records before DVM was established (889 cases).[15]

- Critical reading of all the literature on the Canadian model, changing policy and practice within the criminal justice system in Britain and elsewhere.

---

15 Dianne Butterworth provided invaluable assistance with this.

- In-depth formal and informal interviews with key individuals/agencies in the borough.

- Observation and participation in planning, management and other meetings.

- Regular contact with project staff, including informal observation and discussion of their work, attending some team meetings, and two phased sets of formal in-depth interviews.

- Design of the database on which to record pre- and post-DVM cases. DataEase software, a relational database, was used in order to enable linking new incidents with existing cases and to conduct simple analysis on the data. The database included the incident, police response and that of the DVM workers, and subsequent civil and criminal law actions.

- Training of DVM staff in the use of the data base, maintenance of it, and analysis of the data held within it (1,236 cases, 1,542 incidents).[16]

- Drawing a sample from the data base of incidents where arrest had occurred, following these through police records to CPS files and back to DVM case notes (149 arrests, 72 charges, 34 CPS cases).[17]

- Design, administration, coding and analysis of three phased questionnaires for police officers (502 questionnaires in total).[18] Each questionnaire included several common questions exploring attitudes and responses to domestic violence, others were varied to explore contact with and use of DVM, factors affecting the use of arrest, and the impact of local and national changes in policing on responses to domestic violence.

- Two focus group sessions with officers from each division in early 1995 and several 'ride around' sessions with officers on shift.

- Design, administration, coding and analysis of questionnaires to users of DVM's service and women in the borough withdrawing complaints (229 questionnaires in total). The evaluation questionnaire was lengthy including questions on the history of violence, previous contacts with the police and other agencies, the recent incident, and police and DVM responses to it. A further set of questions was added following comments from the first 30 returns on what additional

---

16 Kate Cook tracked these cases and analysed the data.
17 The design, coding and analysis of all questionnaire data was done collectively by the staff of the Child and Woman Abuse Studies Unit; Sheila Burton, Liz Kelly and Linda Regan.
18 This was resolved in one division by locating investigative officers within the DVU, so that the whole process is located in one office, rather than split between the DVU and crime desks

questions should be included, these focused on how women coped with abuse and how they were coping now.

- Design, coding and analysis of a mid-point follow-up of service users, covering what difference, if any, DVM had made at the time, how important the 'out of hours' service and workers being civilians was, their current situation and whether there had been any subsequent violence (23 interviews).

- Design, administration, coding and analysis of two sets of questionnaires to other agencies in the borough (115 in total) and one set of telephone interviews in mid-1995 (24). The former assessed contact with domestic violence, current referral patterns and inter-agency links, the latter involved contacting agencies most used by DVM to obtain an assessment of the impact of the project locally.

- Design, coding and analysis of a questionnaire to members of the Programme Management Group to explore the structure of the project (4 returns).

- A study trip with other DVM personnel to London, Ontario in summer 1994.

An immense amount of data has been generated and analysed, only a fraction of which can be presented in this report. Much of the detail it has been possible to explore and record in relation to police practice was the direct outcome of the daily interactions between DVM and police officers. The level of access that was possible because the project was based within the police meant that the data generated has a richness and depth that is often lacking in independent research on agency – in this case the police – practice. Many of the complexities which hinder the introduction of new policies and practices could be unravelled, resulting in more detailed criticisms. These should, however, be understood as the outcome of the detailed and ongoing scrutiny that the DVM project enabled. It undoubtedly created a different level of access for the evaluator to the intricacy of the obstacles in implementing consistent law enforcement responses to domestic violence.

There is an evaluation 'story' which echoes the frustrations and complexities for the project as a whole (see Chapter Six). Despite this, however, all the elements which featured in the original tender, along with additions were completed. The most significant hurdles and limitations are discussed in Chapters Three to Five, where the research data is presented.

Several issues need to be noted at this point. The police definition of domestic violence is not the same as the one used by DVM; the latter focuses on abuse by current or ex partners, the former on assaults and disputes between family members. Police data in Islington do not distinguish between these relationships, but the analysis of records before DVM began revealed that, similar to the yearly data published by Greater Manchester Police (GMP, 1994, 1995), assault of current or ex female partners by men constitutes the vast majority (an average of 90%) of all reported cases.

Police record keeping in Islington – as elsewhere (see Grace, 1995; Walker and McNicol 1994) – is not entirely reliable. Despite a force and local policy to record all domestic violence incidents on crime sheets, not all officers have done, or do, this. Additionally both DVUs reported difficulties in maintaining accurate records, particularly with regard to the outcomes of cases after arrest.[19] Despite a number of attempts to resolve these problems within the pilot they remain, resulting in a limitation of outcome data.

Whilst the DVM database accurately records the number of cases in which DVM had a significant input, it does not include advice to other agencies, or telephone enquiries from women who contacted the project independently and provided limited information about themselves. Monitoring of DVM has focused on the number of cases and incidents dealt with, not the number of 'interventions' (a follow up phone call counts as an 'intervention') which FCS count. Initial police responses, and those of DVM are also relatively accurately recorded, but the problems of tracking case outcomes means that the intention of including within the database all legal processes was not achievable. Over the lifetime of the pilot it became obvious that staff members had varying levels of skill and confidence using the software, and on reflection consistency might have been best achieved through one staff member having designated responsibility for it.

The 'action research' element was successful in some respects and not in others. The pressures on the project workers and the management to deal with shorter term 'operational' issues invariably took precedence over longer term reflections and change. But some of the recommendations from each of the interim reports were acted upon, and a number implemented within the three-year pilot.

---

19   Police DVU's report an increase in the number of lesbians and gay men making official complaints about violence in their relationships. This probably reflects an increased confidence in police responses, especially that of DVUs.

3 Making a difference — crisis intervention

"The crisis would have been unbearable without their support"

Three of DVM's aims directly relate to crisis intervention: the establishment of the service to follow up police action; to make contact within 24 hours of police being called; and through the intervention to decrease repeat calls, increase the likelihood of prosecutions being followed through and of referrals to other agencies being taken up.

In this chapter a number of elements of the evaluation data are used to assess DVM's achievement of these aims: the project data base; evaluation questionnaires sent to users and the follow up of cases; agency and police questionnaires; interviews with police officers and support workers and observations in the office. Numeric data are combined with direct quotes to give a flavour of DVM at work and its impacts on individual lives.

What is a crisis?

The definition of crisis underpinning DVM's practice is 'any point at which routine coping strategies break down and the need or potential for change is present'. Calling the police is undoubtedly a crisis in this sense, but so is deciding to tell *anyone* that abuse is occurring and/or seeking medical attention for injuries sustained. Encountering neighbours after the police have been called, or having to explain a partner's behaviour to friends and relatives are also crises. Each involve having to make some kind of public explanation or statement about events which predominantly occur in private. Each contains the potential for support, blame, advice or intervention – the possibility of losing or gaining an opportunity for connection and change.

The responses of others to these crises are more appropriate and effective if they are informed by an awareness of what individuals are coping with, how they are coping currently and what the possibilities for change are. What is said and done at crisis points either enhances the potential for change or pushes someone back into reliance on previous, probably ineffective, coping strategies.

Crisis intervention is directed towards enabling change at some level. 'At some level' is critically important here – change was not conceptualised by DVM solely in terms of leaving or taking legal action against a violent man. Rather it was much more fluid and variable; the basic requirement being *only* that it shift the dynamics of power and control which underpin domestic violence in the woman's favour; ensuring that she had more resources after intervention than before it. This could be personal insight, strengthened resolve, accurate information, access to other agencies, or a firmer alliance with the criminal justice system; often it was a combination. This chapter illustrates how these processes of change occurred for many of the women supported by DVM.

DVM's practice framework recognised that women develop, of necessity, ways to cope with domestic violence. They are active agents, rather than passive victims; learning to read men's behaviour in minute detail, in order to predict what may happen next. They take strategic decisions in which their own safety, that of their children and their self-respect are weighed and considered. They also have to find ways to manage the pain, hurt, betrayals of trust and humiliations which accompany repeated physical, sexual and emotional abuse. How women cope at any one time, or over time is neither fixed or universal; switches from defensive to assertive strategies and back again are not only possible but frequent. Table 3.1 illustrates the most common coping strategies reported by a sample of 166 women supported by DVM (this question was added to the evaluation questionnaire after the first 150 had been sent out). The relevance of these strategies to police responses is discussed below and in Chapter Four.

Table 3.1 Most common strategies used to cope with domestic violence

Coping strategy	Number	Percentage*
Living from day to day	121	73
Try to reason with abuser	112	68
Try to appease abuser	102	61
Minimise abuse/not name it violence	93	56
Make excuses for the abuser's behaviour	80	48
Take the blame oneself	73	44
Change own behaviour	72	43
Refuse some of the abuser's demands	68	41
Drinking/taking prescribed drugs oneself	67	40
Leaving/escaping	65	39
Living for the good times and forgetting the bad	58	35
Finding out about options	51	31

* This was a multiple response question so percentages do not add up to 100, calculated on a base figure of 166.

All of these strategies involve action rather than passivity. The variation in responses between women, and for the same woman over time is but one reason why inflexible models of the impacts of domestic violence, such as Battered Women's Syndrome (see also Kelly, Regan and Burton, 1995; Kelly 1996), are dangerous. Not only do they exclude as much of women's behaviour as they include, but they also establish a normative model against which each woman's behaviour is measured.

Some of the strategies which women use can, from the outside, be seen as not in her and/or her children's longer term interests, and many of them are misunderstood and misinterpreted by others, not least by the police. Several simple examples which have been, and are misread by police officers are: fighting back in words or deeds; resisting controlling behaviour (even though this has, in the past, resulted in worse violence); splitting public and private lives (achieving and being successful in the former at the cost of denying the latter); precipitating an assault which is brewing (in order to end the tension of not knowing when it will happen); using alcohol and/or drugs (as a way of escaping the tension and anxiety). Awareness of the complexity of coping, and how many strategies limit the likelihood of seeking help, or prompt judgemental responses, informed DVM's understanding and practice. For example, encouraging prosecution when a woman is minimising violence and/or blaming herself is unlikely to be effective.

Basic service provision

During the 32 months of direct service provision DVM dealt with a minimum of 1,236 cases and 1,542 incidents (the database does not include 'minimal contact' cases); 362 in Year 1 (8 months of direct service provision, a notional 573 for the full 12 months); 550 in Year 2 (12 months) and 386 in Year 3 (12 months). Whilst the amount of information on cases and incidents varies, some information on each of these is contained in the DVM database. Before looking at DVM's crisis intervention work, some brief details of who the project worked with are in order.

The vast majority of victims were female (99.4%) and perpetrators male (99%), only two cases of female to male violence are recorded, with a small number of lesbian and gay male relationships.[20] The bulk of cases DVM worked with, therefore, involved heterosexual couples where the male was violent to the female. Given the oft repeated question 'why doesn't she leave', the fact that in a third of cases the violence was committed by an ex-partner is both significant and disturbing. Unfortunately for all too many women leaving does not ensure safety.

---

20   789 questionnaires were sent out (women who had minimal contact, who were still living with dangerous partners, who DVM had no current address for, and/or who did not speak English were not sent copies); a return rate of 28%, slightly higher than the estimated 25% in the original tender.

Another significant fact is that 21 per cent of the women DVM worked with were black and a further 10 per cent from ethnic minorities (particularly Turkish and Irish). This not only questions the common assumption that Black and ethnic minority women are less likely to contact the police, but raises a different possibility – that they may call them more often, since these percentages are considerably higher than the black and ethnic minority population of the borough. Clearly further research is needed to explore whether there are two overlapping realities. There has been documentation that sections of ethnic minority communities are deeply distrustful of the police, fearing and anticipating racism. In the case of domestic violence it has been argued that this results in women being reluctant to turn to the police for help (Hague and Malos 1993; Kanuha, 1996; Mama, 1989). Whilst the distrust is undoubtedly there, perhaps it co-exists – at least for some sections of ethnic minority communities – with a frequent resort to the police. Possible explanations may be that the police are the only agency who individuals are aware can be contacted in an emergency, and/or because they are isolated from (or fearful of the reaction of) kin and community. This extensive use of DVM by sections of ethnic minority communities was both encouraging and not anticipated at the outset. Fifty-five (4%) DVM users were disabled women. Some of their impairments created additional needs and complexities, such as sign language interpreters, home visits and the limited availability of accessible, safe, temporary accommodation.

Information from the DVM database in Tables 3.2 to 3.5 outline the referral routes to the project, the times referrals were made and the immediate actions taken by support workers.

Table 3.2   Referral routes to DVM

Referral route	Number	Percentage
Police crisis call	517	42
Self referral	291	23
Police delayed referral	187	15
DVU referral	136	11
Agency/other referral	107	9
TOTAL	1,238	100

Immediate crisis calls comprised 40 per cent for the first two years and 68 per cent for the final year. That increase is, however, in the context of a 30 per cent decrease in overall referrals for the last 12 months. Over two-thirds (70%) of DVM's referrals come directly from the police, and a significant proportion of the 'self referral' route were linked to police leaving DVM referral cards. The intention to follow up police action has, therefore, been achieved, albeit not always at optimal levels.

The number of referrals from NI were twice as many as from NH. Responses from the second and third police questionnaires neither helped explain this difference or the overall drop in referrals. Whilst not all officers completed the question on referrals to DVM in specific time periods, those that did reported substantially higher referral rates than had actually been received. Clearly either officers were over-estimating their referrals or alternatively were making referrals in ways other than the agreed protocol, which never reached DVM.

Table 3.3 illustrates the necessity of 'out of hours' shifts if immediate crisis intervention is to be provided; over two-thirds of DVM's referrals came through outside normal office hours.

Table 3.4 demonstrates that for the majority of referrals a crisis response was possible, be it in person or on the telephone, at the woman's house or the police station; although crisis call outs have never been more than a quarter of the responses. Table 3.5 gives basic information on the kind of immediate interventions DVM provided, and demonstrates the variable combinations of support and advice service users needed.

Table 3.3   Time of DVM call outs*

Time	Year 1 %	Year 2 %	Year 3 %
00.00 – 10.00	24	27	24
10.01 – 18.00	29	28	33
18.01 – 23.59	47	44	42

In this and all subsequent tables using Years 1–3, Year 1 comprises 01/02/93 – 30/09/93 (8 months), Year 2 01/10/93 – 30/09/94 (12 months), Year 3 01/10/94 – 30/09/95 (12 months)

Table 3.4   DVM Immediate Response

Response	Year 1 %	Year 2 %	Year 3 %
Crisis call out	23	25	18
Crisis phone call	19	26	19
Interview at station	21	28	34
Delayed visit	4	1	3
Delayed phone advice	22	17	17
Other	9	2	7

Table 3.5   DVM Actions

Action	Percentage
Support	100
Legal advice	86
Housing advice	60
Crisis planning	30
Other advice	29
Accompany to safe accommodation	15
Counselling advice/referral	13
Accompany for medical treatment	3

The quotes which follow, from the co-ordinator's second quarterly report and interviews with the support workers give a flavour of the content of the work and what they perceive as its advantages.

In 1990, the FCS in Ontario reported that interventions were requiring increasing lengths of time for crisis resolution; 32 per cent of cases involved a worker spending 90 minutes at the scene. The same appears to be true here. Attending a call-out is the beginning of a process which could take hours that same night. The victim may need accompanying to the hospital and is usually too distressed to be left on her own waiting in casualty; she may have children who need to be driven to a place of safety; she may need to be taken to the police station to be seen by the FME [Forensic Medical Examiner] or to give a statement (both processes take a lot of time) or she may request placement in temporary accommodation or a refuge (which can take hours).

Follow-up advocacy with neighbourhood offices (for temporary and permanent accommodation), social workers, solicitors, DSS, police officers and numerous other agencies takes much time over the phone and involves additional paperwork, which is usually in the form of support letters or confirmation of involvement with the client.

The theory of referring people to appropriate outside agencies is workable when such an agency exists, but the diversity and complexity of cases requires overall co-ordination which the team take on if the client is unable to do so herself. Many victims are too distressed to cope with overwhelming bureaucracy or need help filling in forms or have difficulty communicating in English. Some are not on the phone and have small children – it is quicker, kinder and more efficient if we, for instance, make an appointment with the DSS for them rather than insisting that they struggle with baby buggies and feed a lot of money into public call boxes. (DVM Co-ordinator's second quarterly report)

We've got a much more sophisticated approach now from the last three years. I began with not that much experience of domestic violence but having done crisis intervention in a different field of work. Going out to addresses seeing someone very soon after they had been assaulted was very new for me. The ideas behind that kind of work - women are more likely to move on, more likely to seek temporary accommodation - I find that has been happening and that is very satisfying. That approach I find is much better than contacting women hours later, a 9-5 service. That is the brilliant thing about DVM that we can be called out when the incidents are happening.

One of the good things for me is the way women have trusted us - we all had concerns about that coming from a police station. But it is amazing, very quickly women tell of everything that has been happening for her. That enables us to cover lots of areas, and the feedback we get is that women feel very supported because we can link up all their needs - housing, finances, the criminal side. All the information can be provided from one service - so I think one of the strong things is that we provide information about lots of things and work with lots of different agencies.

When we see a woman very soon after the incident it seems to me that they are much more open, much more responsive; within a few hours they often close up and it's much more difficult then to get in until there is another assault. Even if they choose to go back, having talked, they know there is a link there, somewhere to come back to. A lot of women are much more able to say 'do take me out of this situation'. The change that only a few hours makes is very marked. That's why it is a shame that the incidents are happening, but we are not getting as many immediate referrals as we used to do. (SW4)

I think we can link things up for women. If they think they have to go to six agencies to sort things out that can be a reason for thinking 'I can't cope with all this right now'. Whilst we can't deal with everything, we can inform and talk through all the issues and options. Being able to network, go with someone, refer to the right person makes it much easier than having to do all that leg work themselves when they are feeling very vulnerable. It's striking the balance between working with the woman so that she can help herself. But when she has just been assaulted she's very vulnerable. Often women say 'I don't feel confident enough to make that phone call, to go to that service'. Just making the phone call can make such a difference. (SW3)

I see crisis intervention as getting to women when their defences are down. Something has happened to them, and they can probably see things a bit clearer, they are asking 'what's going on?' You can help them to clear away some of the debris, some of the lies that they have taken on board. If they are in a coping situation, they are coping. In practical terms we can provide help immediately, provide back up to the police, we can find them a safe place, and that can make such a difference. It may be that the woman isn't ready to move on - that's fine, we will do what they need then. I think if women come direct to us, they are connecting with domestic violence and are ready to make some kind of move, but they are not sure what it will involve. I had a woman come in the other day, she came to offer to be a volunteer. She'd had contact last year. She was a young woman and I looked up her file, and she had been badly assaulted. She turned up, she looked great, she's going back to college, got her own flat, She'd got her own life together and she wanted to put something back in. We talked about life after domestic violence; so that's a real success story and she put a lot of it down to DVM. Then there are people you just know are getting on with things - they ring up to say they've moved, or to say they are ok. Then there are women in ongoing situations who find it very difficult to get out. There's a woman at the moment trying to get into detox, she's got so many problems, and she is leaning on us to help with sorting out the complexities of all of it. I don't think she's going to leave him at the moment, but she's getting her life together in other areas and we can help her in that. (SW1)

The initial views of the DVU officers in both divisions - that it was better to wait until the immediate crisis has past - are questioned by the experience of the support workers, and the opinions of DVM's users (see later).

Table 3.6   Repeat attacks

Number of reported incidents	Pre-DVM police data (6 months)		DVM data (32 months)	
	N	%	N	%
1	691	78	1,030	67
2	49	5	134	9
3	11	1	34	2
4	4		13	1
5	1		3	
6	3		3	
7	2		2	
8			2	
13			1	
14	1		1	
TOTAL	889		1,542	

The DVM database also enables some assessment of the intention to decrease repeat calls to the police and for DVM to respond within 24 hours of the incident. The six monthly pre-DVM police data provided a repeat attack figure of 22 per cent, with 11 per cent making three or more calls within six months. Table 3.6 records the pre-DVM police data and DVM's repeat attack figures for a period of 32 months – five times the length of time for the comparison data. Whilst one would not expect the figures to be five times as big at 19 months, only 25 per cent had reported a repeat attack, and the figure was 33 per cent at the full 32 months. The proportion making three or more calls is even more significant at 15 per cent for the entire pilot, and the figures for six or more reported incidents are exactly the same, although the DVM time period is five times that of the police data. An additional indication of success in decreasing repeat attacks is the proportion of women returning the evaluation questionnaires who have called the police before. The proportion in the first batch analysed was two-thirds, this had decreased to 40 per cent for the last 61. The detailed breakdown for prior calls to the police for three time periods with the most recent batch first are: once (28%, 25%, 21%); several times (45%, 46%, 37%); many occasions (20%, 25%, 42%). These data offer support to DVM's aim to reduce 'recidivism', suggesting that DVM's interventions are more likely to produce a resolution, rather than a temporary respite.

Nonetheless DVM have had repeat contacts with some women. Crisis intervention on a regular basis with the same person can take different, and at times no doubt frustrating, forms. Here again the project has developed skill, expertise and understandings which others could learn from.

Some of what we are doing is laying groundwork, so women know we are here and can come back and say 'yes you are right something has to really change'.... She will come to prosecution, but she needs support, a stable agency that she can ring at night when the next crisis happens.

There is a lot of phoning in the evening just to have someone to talk to, to tell about a recent crisis, for interim advice, because of depression. Once women have left partners there is a lull and, for some, terrible depression and loneliness and just telling someone can help. Different women want different things.

What I do is work on a strategy for coping, map it, asking things like how long ago was the last incident, how many have there been, and as we go through it sometimes something just clicks. They often say 'it's happened more times than I realised' and I say 'it's a bit like being in a boxing ring, you get punch drunk'. One of the things I also say is that if you are being injured your threshold of pain is gone, you don't even know how much pain you are subjected to, and it's dangerous. (SW2)

Taking time to explore the history and changes in violence is not something police are able to do, due to time constraints and their statutory responsibility to investigate whether a crime has been committed. What DVM has shown is that for a significant proportion of women, space to explore their experience is precisely what enables them to develop a perspective, to shift from coping day to day.

The aim of DVM to make contact within 24 hours was achieved in an average of 90 per cent of cases throughout the pilot with the percentage increasing over time from an initial 88 per cent to 92 per cent in the final year. At least a third of contacts are made immediately following an incident. Delayed contact occurs for a number of reasons: the police referral itself is delayed; women choosing to wait until the next day before speaking to someone and the other referral routes not occurring as a result of a recent incident. From the standpoint of crisis theory, however, women approaching an outside agency at any point represents a disruption of routine coping strategies and is itself a form of crisis.

The support workers were asked in interviews to discuss what they regarded as DVM's success in terms of crisis intervention.

There are a lot of cases which show what we can do. Some women have been in contact with us from the beginning and they are now out of that situation, but that took a year, year and a half and a lot of contact. We have quite a lot of women who have done that. It's difficult to measure success in domestic violence, but I think it's good if women are out of the situation, safe and protected. We have also had cases – one last week – where the perpetrator has got a custodial sentence. This woman is now back at work and she wrote us a brilliant letter saying her life had turned around. (SW3)

There was consensus that one essential element to success was not defining a crisis too restrictively.

A question for me is where do you actually limit the intervention – how much ongoing support do you give? We've given a lot of support to some women; you build up quite a rapport, you can see women through quite a lot. The conclusion I've come to is that just being a referral agency and pulling strands together is not enough. Not in counselling or social work case load terms, but keeping the threads together supporting the next steps. It pays off in terms of the woman having the confidence to see it through. The crisis isn't just the incident, it has lots of sub-sections later on. (SW4)

Assessment of DVM crisis intervention by users

The basic DVM data and the accounts of the staff team suggest that the crisis intervention element of the project has been an unqualified success – with the caveat that police referrals dropped significantly in the final year of the pilot. The outstanding question is whether the experience of women using the project supports this conclusion. The next section draws on the responses of the 223[21] who completed evaluation questionnaires and the follow up monitoring exercise done in 1994. The questionnaire data have been analysed for the whole group and over three time periods to assess whether there were any significant changes over the pilot.

Two of the returns are from men, with 221 from women; all of the perpetrators were male with the single exception of a female abuser in a lesbian relationship. The questionnaires were completed at varying intervals after contact with DVM: 32 per cent within the week; 30 per cent within 1 to 4 weeks; and 38 per cent more than a month later. More basic demographic data is available on this group than on the database, but comparisons have been made to assess how representative of DVM service users those who returned the questionnaires were. The youngest was 18 and the oldest 81, with 43 per cent being under 30. Over a third define themselves as being from an ethnic minority group, with 21 per cent being Black or mixed race; African-Caribbean origins are a more significant proportion than Asian (this fairly closely parallels the database information). Over two-thirds of the women had children living with them. Sixty-four per cent were abused by a current partner and 36 per cent by ex-partners (again a similar distribution to that in the database).

At the time they completed the questionnaire only 15 per cent (32) were living with the abusive partner (compared to 50 per cent at the time of the incident), and five of this group were not intending this to be permanent. A further 15 per cent (32) had moved into safe/alternative accommodation and for 29 per cent (62) their male partners had left/been excluded from the home. The remaining 36 per cent (79) had not been living with the perpetrator at the time and still were not. This is the one difference with the database, women completing the evaluation questionnaires were more likely to have left their partners. Of women moving to safe housing, the majority had gone to hotels, bed and breakfast and local reception centres with a minority finding a place in a refuge. A noticeable shift occurred during the pilot, with less refuge and temporary accommodation places being found and an increase in alternatives (such as excluding the man, staying with friends/relatives), perhaps reflecting the pressure on temporary accommodation locally.

---

21   789 questionnaires were sent out (women who had minimal contact, who were still living with dangerous partners, who DVM had no current address for, and/or who did not speak English were not sent copies); a return rate of 28%, slightly higher than the estimated 25% in the original tender.

In order to assess what kind of difference DVM made data were collected on the history of the violence and previous help-seeking (including from the police but that data appears in the next chapter).

Women's experiences of abuse

Tables 3.7 and 3.8 report the number of incidents of violence which women had experienced before the most recent one, and the forms of violence which they had been subject to on more than one occasion. Changes worth noting here over the course of the pilot are, the emergence of a small group who report no physical assaults, but where threats and persistent mental cruelty had occurred, and an increase in the proportion of women reporting over 60 assaults from six per cent to nine per cent.

Table 3.7   Extent of violence

Number of assaults	N	%
No physical violence	15	7
Less than 10	105	48
11–20	45	20
21–40	24	11
41–60	10	5
More than 60	20	9
Non-response	4	2

Table 3.8 lists the percentages of women experiencing various forms of violence, and compares them with findings from a small scale prevalence study, using GPs' surgeries as a contact point, conducted in 1989 (McGibbon et al. (1989), in Hammersmith and Fulham – 48 per cent of this group of women had experienced violence or threats from a male partner, compared to the 100 per cent in the DVM sample.

Table 3.8   Women experiencing abuse on more than two occasions*

Form of abuse	DVM %	H&F %
Threats of violence	93	29
Repeated criticism	91	48
Slaps/punches	89	35
Damage to property	84	-
Beating	63	18
Strangulation	53	-
Threats to kill	47	13
Forced sex	45	13
Assaults with weapons	39	10

*   This was a multiple response question, percentages calculated on base figure of 223 for the DVM sample and 281 for the Hammersmith and Fulham study.

Interestingly over the life of the pilot there were significant increases in the proportions reporting all forms listed apart from repeated criticism and threats to kill, both of which increased slightly. At the same time the frequency of assaults decreased, raising the possibility that a proportion of women were seeking help at an earlier point. It is also clear that the DVM women had experienced more extensive violence than the Hammersmith and Fulham general population group, even taking into account the differential distribution of ever suffering violence across the two groups.

Just under half of the women who had ever been pregnant were assaulted whilst they were pregnant, and 25 per cent of this group said the violence affected the pregnancy. This included six women reporting miscarriages, a further four threatened miscarriages, five premature births, and three babies in intensive care. Two women told poignant stories of repeated miscarriages due to assaults.

The majority of women with children (84%) reported that their children had witnessed and/or overheard the violence, and in just over half of the cases children had attempted to intervene to protect their mothers (if we take into account that some children were too young to do this, then the proportion of older children intervening is much higher). In 19 cases at least one child was also assaulted attempting to protect their mother, and in another 19 cases women were aware of abuse of children separate to that they were experiencing. Only 22 (15%) felt that their children had not been affected by the violence, although a further 43 (27%) were not sure.

Previous help-seeking

Under half (40%) had called the police on previous occasions. Over half (55%) of those who had called the police previously were happy with their response, 16 per cent were never happy and 30 per cent reported variable responses. Thus not only are there differences between women but the same women have contrasting experiences on different occasions (more details on this are presented in the next chapter). Just under a third had also applied for injunctions previously. Almost half of this group of women had taken actions to limit violence and obtain protection, none of which had been effective in changing the man's behaviour.

Contrary to popular opinion, very few women had not talked to anyone about the violence (17, 8%). As previous research has documented (McGibbon, Cooper and Kelly, 1989; Mooney, 1994) women were most likely to turn to their friends and relatives, predominantly although not exclusively female friends, and the vast majority reported the responses as helpful. The most frequently mentioned forms of support were: listening and not being judgemental; advice; being there on a day to day basis; offering safety when needed. That said, however, 70 per cent of this group had never approached a formal agency – other than the police – about their abuse, and of the remaining 30 per cent half had only made one such approach.

> *I felt too ashamed especially as I kept taking him back; they would not understand why when they knew what had been going on.*

> *Stupidly I never thought it was serious enough.*

The factors which most commonly prevented this contact were: not knowing support existed; not thinking their situation was serious enough; fear; shame/protection of privacy.

Contact with and assessment of DVM

Table 3.9 records women's initial responses to the idea of DVM. Only 10 per cent were not able to see/speak to a DVM worker very quickly, with 35 per cent involving a home visit and 26 per cent an in-person meeting at the police station. This immediate contact was perceived to make a difference by most women (82%).

Table 3.9   Initial responses to the idea of DVM

Response	Number	Percentage*
Relief – to talk to someone	122	56
Unsure what to expect	82	38
Hope could answer questions	61	28
Interested	58	27
Worried they might pry	13	7
Worried they might blame	12	6

*   This was a multiple response question, percentages calculated on base of 223.

Women's accounts of what difference it made offer further support for the theory of crisis intervention; 151 provided specific examples of the importance of immediate support. The predominant themes were having space to talk and explore their feelings and options, and reassurance coupled with increased confidence that they could and even should act in the interests of their own safety.

If more time had lapsed I probably wouldn't have talked to anyone about it.

If the response had not been immediate I would probably have taken him back.

I am more aware of the fact that domestic violence is not acceptable in any circumstances.

I didn't think my boyfriend was actually being violent until she pointed a few things out.

I got on immediately with the practical matters of divorce and joint tenancy, I didn't stop to hesitate.

I thought it was all my fault but after speaking and listening I realised he had more of a problem.

I accepted a lot for a long time because I didn't want anyone to know and just put a face on for everyone, but I think I would tell friends now.

The importance of space to talk, exploring the meaning of abuse were confirmed by responses to a question about what individuals wanted from DVM (Table 3.10); these needs far exceed concerns about arrest and prosecution, although these did increase somewhat over the lifetime of the pilot project.

Table 3.10 What victims wanted from DVM

	Number	Percentage
To talk about recent events	138	62
Advice	113	51
Support that abuse is unacceptable	109	49
To discuss prosecution options	39	17
To discuss implications of arrest	29	13
Explore how to end the relationship	24	11
Discuss how to get partner to change	17	10

*   This was a multiple response question, percentages calculated on base of 223.

The vast majority thought DVM had provided what they wanted, although there were 22 dissenting voices. Their complaints were (in order of frequency mentioned): no reliable protection/safety; more immediate and personal contact than was possible at the time; support about health issues; more understanding and more information.

The support workers were perceived remarkably positively throughout the whole pilot, with only a marginal decrease in glowing comments in the final year. More than three-quarters of service users (80%) said that there was something in particular that the DVM workers said that they found helpful. The most frequently mentioned were: that DVM could offer follow-up support; the amount of advice and referral information – particularly the existence of refuges/safe accommodation; that violence was not acceptable; that they were not to blame. Only eight referred to unhelpful statements which were: that the man would never change; one option would be to buy her own council house; and being told that the final decision in terms of a prosecution for breach of an injunction would be up to a judge. Whilst the critical comments should be taken seriously, very few constitute complaints about what the support workers said or did, and most refer to issues beyond the remit/control of DVM.

The support DVM offered in terms of arrest and prosecution is dealt with in the next chapter. Whilst the proportion of referrals to other agencies which were taken up by women completing the evaluation questionnaire (an average of a third) is lower than that reported by FCS, it is significant, nonetheless, since hardly any of the woman had used these resources previously. This also needs to placed in the context of a far more limited range of agencies locally devoted to domestic violence.

Women were asked if DVM had offered and provided follow-up support; the vast majority of commitments to follow-ups by DVM were done within two days of initial contact (for 66% of the sample), a further 68 women (just under a third) had made contact themselves in the week after first contact. The content of follow-up contact varied between straightforward checks to see how women were, to quite complex requests for advice, practical and emotional support.

When asked to rate the DVM support workers response, 63 per cent said they were extremely helpful, and the remaining 36 per cent rated them as either very or quite helpful and 1 per cent (3) as not very helpful. Three-quarters said that the contact with DVM had made a difference, 17 per cent were not sure and 8 per cent (19) that it had no impact. How DVM had made a difference for this group of women represents a clear reminder about the importance of basic principles. What mattered most was clear messages that abuse/violence was not acceptable, that women were not to blame, and that they had a right to lives free of violence. After over two decades of publicity and media attention it is easy to presume that few victims of domestic violence would blame themselves, but that is to neglect what we know about the content and dynamics of abusive relationships, where women's sense of reality and self can be profoundly distorted. It is the certainty with which DVM workers communicated these basic messages which provided the basis for the next most important element for women – increasing their confidence and belief in themselves. It is on these two bases that options and advice become meaningful.

> *She helped me understand that no-one has the right to do those things and get away with it.*

> *It was very important that I was able to talk to a stranger and not feel looked down on. I feel more confident now about calling the police.*

> *Having a strong woman say that I'll be ok, that I'm not alone made all the difference.*

From this group of 223, responses to an open ended question on how DVM made a difference included 27 explicit statements that without DVM's support women would not have ended the relationship, 20 that in any future incidents the police will be called and prosecution supported, and nine women who would have withdrawn from prosecutions. These are minimal estimates since many women made general, rather than specific comments.

> *I've been running from my ex-husband for six years and I never knew that I was entitled to help and have certain rights..... I am not afraid, it's not my fault and I'm worth more than violence and abuse.*

> *Well I got away from a psycho, I could not ask for any more than that.*

It gave me the courage to be strong and fight for what was my right to care for my family without abuse... I now feel I have more choices, and therefore more control over my problem. I'm dealing with it now so he'd better watch it. He'll never abuse me again.

Without her help I would not have charged him.

If it wasn't for them I would still be in my old flat, I would have forgiven him because I would have been frightened not to. Things would have been back to square one.

I finally got the courage to get out of the situation.

There was a woman with experience on hand almost 24 hours a day! Almost everything [surprised me]. They have time for you, they listen, they let you sound off, give good advice, don't judge you and generally try and make you feel good about yourself without pitying you.... I don't feel as confident as I did and I don't trust men at the moment. I feel like I have let myself down by letting him abuse me for so long. So now I have to start again. That's a bit scary, but I feel like I can do it. The hardest thing was walking away from someone that I care about who was abusing me. I have done that, so I guess I have taken the first step.

I'm starting all over again for myself and my daughter and I can guarantee that I'll never be in this situation again because I'll never let it happen. I feel much stronger and I'll always be strong. After all I've got my life and I want it to be well lived, but without blackouts and bruises. At the end of the day I've been lucky in that it hasn't affected me badly. I've had the stress and the pain of everything, but now I've had help and support. I just want to forget everything about him.

The questionnaire concluded with questions about women's current situation, which highlighted that even if women are able to end relationships and violence, they are often still left struggling to make sense of and come to terms with that history. Within this, however, women made statements about re-discovering what it was like to live free from fear and abuse, and talked with excitement about "finding myself again" and being "determined to make something of my life". Responses to this series of questions revealed the courage and determination it requires of women, not just to act in relation to violence, but to maintain their resolve over time. There were many moving comments about loneliness, loss of trust, loss of home, friends and community, as well as assessments of the damage abuse had done to women's physical and mental health.

Follow-up monitoring with service users was done for two groups in late 1994 – all who had been in contact with DVM in November 1993 and May 1994 to get a six- and twelve-month gap. A short interview schedule was drawn up which covered: reflections on the service they had received; what difference, if any, DVM's availability outside office hours, the support workers being women and civilians made; their current situation; and whether there had been any further violence. Interviews were conducted on the telephone. Contact was made, and agreement to participate was given, by 23 women (a significant proportion of the listings could not be traced, or were not reachable by telephone). Fourteen had been supported by DVM 12 months previously, nine six months ago. In terms of the DVM crisis intervention, six had had a home visit, nine had telephone support and eight were seen at the police station. The majority said the form of support was what they wanted at the time, but five would have preferred a home visit, including a woman whose first language was not English and who found the telephone difficult. Over half had themselves made further contact with DVM and slightly less said DVM had contacted them a second time. Twenty (87%) thought that DVM had made a difference at the time.

Definitely, I could tell them things I couldn't tell my parents, I could be open about everything.

It meant I made that initial step to change my life because they increased my confidence in myself.

Almost the same number thought DVM's availability was important to them, mentioning it made them feel safer/more secure knowing that they could make contact if and when they needed to. Over 75 per cent thought that the workers being women made it easier for them to talk, and for 60 per cent the fact that they were civilians was also important.

I find it easier to talk to women about sensitive issues.

I didn't feel isolated.

They are more understanding of the issues.

Uniforms alert the neighbours to your problems.

They were more attentive, the police did not advise and played down the situation.

It was more informal and I was able to relax.

These responses are echoed by findings reported by Morley and Mullender (1994, p18) where a study of follow up by DVU officers or uniformed officers found that victims preferred the DVU, and did not respond as well to uniformed officers; they note similar findings in Hanmer and Saunders' (1990) research within West Yorkshire.

The most valued things women got from DVM were (in rank order): practical support; emotional support/space to talk; legal advice; assurance that violence was not her fault; that she deserved something better; that what was happening was violence; referrals to other agencies.

Only five women were currently living with their abusive partner, and all maintained that there had been no violence since contact with DVM. All of the five women who reported further violence or threats were separated from the man at the time. All of the three cases involving additional assaults had been reported to the police, but neither of the women who had been threatened had reported. Two women said they would not contact DVM again, but gave no reason for this. The rest said they would if they needed to, and echoed the questionnaire responses.

> *I have no complaints whatsoever. I'm glad they were there and I'm glad they made the first move as I wouldn't have been able to.*

In both sets of data some suggestions for improving DVM's service were offered:

- an area for children to play whilst the support worker is speaking to the woman, as children's presence was distracting and distressing;

- regular routine follow ups;

- more support attending solicitors and agencies;

- additional counselling support.

Whilst several of these suggestions fall outside DVM's crisis intervention brief, the responses show that women continue to value the same things over time: personal contact with a female civilian who is able to combine advice with immediate emotional support. The importance of home visits and follow ups illustrate very clearly that pro-active responses are neither resented by women nor ineffectual; rather they appear to accelerate a process of change in a manner which both at the time and retrospectively are valued positively.

The support workers were also aware of areas where further development was needed.

I wish we had been able to produce more information in community languages. We only have access to interpreting 9-5, and the officers going out on call, what support can they give? One really clear example for me of how important this is was a woman being brought to the station and I was told she needed temporary accommodation because she had been assaulted. I was trying to say that we shouldn't be using her child as interpreter, but that's what was happening. It turned out after my insistence that we got an interpreter that she had been burgled, it wasn't domestic violence at all! (SW2)

Towards a model of crisis intervention

To do effective crisis intervention involves developing both awareness and skills to assess each individual woman's current situation – not just the extent of abuse she is suffering but also how she copes with and makes sense of it. A brief outline of some of these processes and some of the implications for crisis intervention is presented below. Models are, by definition, unable to encompass the complexity and messiness of daily life; what follows should not be read as a linear process against which an individual woman's circumstances or 'progress' can be measured. Rather it outlines a contextual framework within which women make decisions.

Managing the situation

The point at which violence is first experienced is a crisis for the relationship, and although some women end relationships at this point, the majority do not. They find, or accept, an explanation for the incident which allows for a future. The next few incidents may test this or reinforce it, especially if it involves believing that it is things she does which 'provoke' violence. What develops are strategies to manage the situation, most commonly to manage the environment and him in order to limit the potentials for conflict. Incidents of abuse and their consequences also have to be managed. Crisis intervention at this point focuses on enabling women to recognise how they are adapting and limiting their behaviour in an attempt to avoid abuse.

Distortion of perspective/reality

Gradually more and more of women's daily life, routines and thought processes are affected by the fact of, and having to manage, violence. Managing anxiety, trying to make sense of why, take up more of her energy and attention. Answering why often involves taking responsibility, both because abusive men are past masters at shifting responsibility, and because some of the strategies women use involve, at least on the level of appearances, accepting that aspects of their behaviour prompt violent outbursts. Managing and coping are increasingly focused on trying to do and not do certain things, or defiantly continuing to act in certain ways, knowing the consequences will be abuse. Either approach means repeated abuse can be understood – by herself and others – as yet again her responsibility. The key issue for crisis intervention here is addressing blame explicitly, exploring why and how women blame themselves, acknowledging the many ways they have tried to change themselves, their environment, and how (un)successful these strategies have been, and what the costs of continuing to live with violence are.

Defining abuse

It is often only after a number of assaults that women define abuse as violence. The mechanisms and meanings involved are complex, since this is not just about using the word violence, but locating oneself as someone who is being victimised and one's partner as an abuser. On some level responsibility has to be placed with the abuser for this to occur, and events understood as a recurring feature in the relationship, rather than occasional aberrations. Crisis intervention names violence explicitly, whilst allowing space for the difficulty and confusion this may create. A key component is often unpicking the exclusionary stereotypes of 'battered women' and 'violent men'.

Re-evaluating the relationship

Once the relationship is understood as one in which abuse/violence occurs a re-evaluation process begins, and whilst the decision to remain, and the strategies used to cope, may continue they are taking place in a changed context of meaning. The possibility of leaving temporarily or permanently, of engaging in formal processes to limit and contain violence become easier to contemplate. Here crisis intervention shifts to exploring what the barriers to ending the relationship are. At issue will be concern about protection, practical and material issues such as housing and income support, loyalty and loss of friends and kin, and whether a network of support can be built to bolster the taking of difficult decisions.

Ending the relationship

Most woman make many attempts to leave violent relationships before they eventually do, and the reasons for returning encompass: believing in promises to change; the absence of acceptable practical alternatives; pressure from relatives, friends and sometimes children; the absence of effective protection. The issues involved will be more complicated for black, migrant, disabled, elderly and lesbian women. Crisis intervention attempts to build a realistic picture of what combination of emotional and practical resources are needed to make the difference, both to make the break and sustain it over time.

Ending the violence

Contrary to popular myth, ending a relationship does not always ensure that violence ends; it may in fact place women at greater risk of serious, and even fatal assault (Daly and Wilson, 1993). Crisis intervention must take seriously women's assessment of the danger they face, using tools like crisis planning, working on building a web of protective factors around her. One element in this will be enabling her to take legal action in relation to subsequent acts of violence.

The movement of any particular woman through these processes can be astonishingly swift, or agonisingly slow, and every point in between. Some women spend years managing and coping in isolation, others seek support quickly. What skilled crisis intervention does is move the process on.

> *I do think that we can make things happen quicker for women. Their frustration is that they are often pushed around to various agencies, sitting for hours and any kind of spirit to do something about it disappears. The less amount of time they have to do that the better, because they are already in crisis and haven't got much energy. The co-ordination is often lacking and we can do some of that.* (SW1)

What women supported by DVM valued was having access to immediate and sympathetic support, the space to talk and explore their feelings and options; reassurance and increased confidence that they could and even should act in the interests of their own safety. Crisis intervention is, however, more than listening – it is pro-active, encouraging women to move on – either in how they make sense of what is happening, how seriously they take it, or increasing the protective and material resources they have access to. It involves supporting the part of the woman which knows her situation is dangerous, is unjust and challenging the internalisation of blame, unworthiness, and the ways their abuser has defined their reality.

The quotes from women earlier in this chapter showed the importance for some women in shifting their understanding/perspective; they were defining violence, allocating responsibility appropriately, questioning and re-evaluating the relationship. For many these were major shifts in perception, but they are seldom regarded or measured as positive outcomes: 'performance indicators'. Other women were at different points in the process, and therefore received and took different things from DVM such as ways to end the relationship, and carrying prosecutions through.

Too often the support offered women presumes the first four stages in the process, and is directed only at ending the relationship; assuming this will end the violence. Presuming rather than exploring the kind of support women need means that what is offered is frequently inappropriate and experienced as patronising, judgemental or irrelevant. It can even reinforce a sense of responsibility, since one is failing to act on the advice proffered.

Any kind of intervention – be it by a friend or police officer – should involve a mutual agreement that something needs to happen/change, at the same time as recognising that the woman herself will have done many things already to limit/control violence. Her confusions and anxieties also need to be recognised. For example, if a woman is unsure whether what she is experiencing is violence, asking questions about how anxious she is, how much she has changed her behaviour will enable clarification. Alternatively if violence is recognised but the woman wants to discuss if the relationship can be saved, discussing how many promises to change have been made, whether violence is more frequent and 'serious' will enable an assessment of the danger she is in.

Skilled crisis intervention backs up these explorations of meaning with practical information and options, to encourage and maintain momentum towards change. It also involves encouraging women to build networks of support around themselves.

Too often agencies expect women to move from confusion to resolute action within short periods of time – but very few of us end intimate relationships so easily and promptly. This model of crisis intervention takes seriously the importance of unpicking layers of internalised responsibility and taken for granted/common sense understandings of domestic violence, since these often constitute barriers to other levels of change. Most professionals will argue that they do not have time to do this detailed work – but if they added up the repeat visits, prescriptions, demands on services an argument for skilled, focused crisis intervention makes long term sense, both financially and in terms of effectiveness. This is undoubtedly one of the key lessons from DVM.

4 Policing and law enforcement

In this chapter DVM's achievements in relation to policing and law enforcement are evaluated with respect to establishing the principle that domestic violence is a crime: "to this end the project workers will encourage action to be taken against the perpetrators and help ensure the protection of victims whilst addressing their ongoing needs" (the support of victims has already been addressed in Chapter Three). Considerable emphasis was placed on encouraging and enhancing law enforcement in the planning and initial phases of the pilot, with core members of the Management Committee being drawn from criminal justice agencies (the CPS participating as observers). A sub-aim in relation to policing was to decrease police time spent at domestic violence calls.

In this chapter pre- and post-DVM police data, the DVM database, the follow through of cases to the CPS, women users questionnaires, the series of questionnaires with police officers and interview data from police and support workers are utilised to explore the complex issues involved. The chapter begins with a discussion of basic data on police responses, followed by the case tracking through the criminal justice system and an assessment of police responses by DVM users. The final major section uses data from police officers to explore the remaining barriers to developing consistent and pro-law enforcement responses.

A set of practice guidelines for police locally were agreed at an early point; they both encouraged a law enforcement orientation to domestic violence and set out the formal links between DVM and the police. DVM was to be called out where arrests were made, in the hope that focused support would enable more women to pursue prosecution, and offered to all other victims.

Police data pre- and post-DVM

One obvious measure of changes in policing practice are arrest and charging rates. These were to be assessed through comparison of pre- and post-DVM police records. Compiling the pre-DVM data from DVU records was both time-consuming and frustrating; two different systems existed and some of the data needed (such as time spent on calls) was simply not available, and other data, such as the outcome of charges and prosecutions, not routinely recorded. Only cases involving 'partnership' violence were included, resulting in a lower incidence locally than that included in the original PDU bid.

Table 4.1 presents data from the analysis of police records from the two divisions (NI and NH) for the six months prior to DVM start date; the 12 month figures at the bottom of the table have been extrapolated by doubling the six monthly figures. The four columns record: the overall number of incidents; incidents where the perpetrator was not present when police arrived; whether the incident was recorded as a crime; and arrests. The figures for arrest are calculated in two ways: as a percentage of the incidents reported (Arrest 1), and as a percentage of the incidents which were recorded as crimes (Arrest 2).[22] Police do respond to domestic violence calls where no 'arrestable offence' has occurred; thus calculating arrest rates on all incidents may be misleading. It is important to appreciate that it proved impossible to track every domestic violence case reported to the police. The problems in collecting accurate data retrospectively have already been noted, these were complicated during the project by sectorisation. Attempts to obtain the data from the police were unsuccessful although some were gathered during the project (see Tables 4.3 to 4.5). The DVM database thus comprises only those cases which were referred to the project. It should also be noted that the project protocol stated that, where arrests occurred, these cases would be automatically referred to DVM. This may mean that the arrest rate in the DVM database is likely to be higher than for all reported cases in the borough. Nor should the DVM database figure be read as an accurate measure of the incidence of reported domestic violence in the borough, since not all cases were referred to the project. This bedevils any comparisons between the two data sets. They are, nonetheless, the best approximations achievable in these circumstances.

Table 4.1   Pre-DVM comparison police action for the two divisions

	Incidents	Perp not present		Crimed		Arrests 1		Arrests 2	
	N	N	%	N	%	N	%	N	%
NI	432	97	22	146	34	56	13	56	38
NH	457	103	22	187	41	67	15	67	36
Total	889	200	22	333	37	123	14	123	37
12 month extrapolation	1,778	400	22	666	37	246	14	246	37

---

22 Note that these data are not the total of police cases, but are confined to cases which were referred or known to DVM; the former would be a much higher figure.

Several important points arise from the comparison data:

- whilst it was policy across both divisions for all domestic violence cases to be recorded on crime sheets, this was only common practice at NH;

- there was a higher 'criming' rate at NH, and a slightly higher arrest rate where the base is incidents (Arrests 1), but not where the arrest rate is calculated on only those cases which are crimed (Arrests 2);

- almost two-thirds of domestic violence incidents were not recorded as crimes;

- of the total arrests, charges were laid in less than half (47%), and this is just over a sixth of the offences which were crimed.

Table 4.2 presents data on the same variables for the 32 months in which the DVM pilot provided direct service.

Table 4.2   DVM data base police action for the two divisions

	Incidents	Perp not present		Crimed		Arrests 1		Arrests 2	
	N	N	%	N	%	N	%	N	%
NI	746	222	30	321	44	196	26	196	61
NH	332	104	31	133	41	89	26	89	67
Total	1,078	326	31	454	42	285	26	285	63

Additional issues are raised by comparing the figures from the two tables.

- In a significant proportion of cases in both tables (up to a third) the perpetrator is not present when police arrive. This means he cannot be arrested, cautioned or even spoken to. Whilst calling police may interrupt assaults, the absence of the perpetrator makes it far less likely that any further action will occur. It is possible for officers to instigate a 'circulated as wanted' procedure, whereby an arrest warrant is issued, but this hardly ever happens in relation to domestic violence. The inclusion of investigative officers in DVUs is one strategy which could address this.

- A higher proportion of cases were crimed in the DVM data set.

- If the arrest rate is recalculated to only cover cases where the perpetrator was present it rises to 18 per cent for the pre-DVM data and 37 per cent for the DVM data base cases. The increase is even more marked if only those cases which were crimed are included; a shift from 37 per cent to 63 per cent.

To test whether the DVM database contained a higher percentage of arrests (since these were the cases which were supposed to be prioritised in police referrals to the project) both divisions were asked to produce incidence and arrest figures for the years 1992 to 1994. These were only produced by NH and appear in Table 4.3.[23] The arrest rate here can only be calculated for incidents, since the figures for 'crimed' cases were not made available.

Table 4.3 Incidence of domestic violence and arrests 1992–1994 NH division

Year	Incidents	Arrests	
		N	*%*
1992	1,488	266	18
1993	1,396	168	13
1994	1,332	252	19

Following recommendations in the second interim evaluation report a senior officer in both divisions monitored domestic violence calls in January 1995. The results are presented below in Table 4.4.

Table 4.4 Police monitoring of domestic violence cases January 1995

Station	Incidents	Arrests	
		N	*%*
NI	59	11	19
NH	117	15	12

The data on the levels of arrests is equivocal, varying according to what data set and what base it is calculated from. There is more evidence of an increase at NI – the station in which DVM was based, and this is paralleled by a decrease of domestic violence calls to NI over the pilot. In the pre-DVM data NI had 5 per cent less cases than NH, for the first six months of 1994

---

23 Data produced throughout the pilot by the police covering similar time periods is not internally consistent. It proved impossible to track these inconsistencies since officers who created earlier sets were no longer working in the division.

this had increased to 12 per cent less and for the second half to 37 per cent less. Whilst there are ongoing concerns about loss of cases which are not being recorded on crime sheets, that is unlikely to account for all of the decrease. Given that DVM worked with significantly more NI cases and was considered by both support workers and police officers to have had more influence in changing practice in the NIDVU/VPU (see Chapter Six) some of this decrease is likely to be due to their intervention - i.e. that cases were resolved at an earlier point, meaning there were less repeat calls.

A key theme in both interim evaluation reports was the limited movement on the law enforcement element of DVM's aims. Additional data were compiled to demonstrate this to police managers. Both DVUs were asked to complete logs over a period of months. Only one was completed by NH. It recorded 86 cases (3 advice only, 35 disputes, 2 breaches of orders and 46 domestic violence) from which 11 arrests were made, three cautions issued, and one charge laid. Whilst caution is needed in relation to the outcome figures, the arrest figures are accurate: in less than a quarter of the cases where an offence was recorded (the 46 domestic violence cases) was an arrest made.

Further evidence that neither the force nor divisional policy on law enforcement was being consistently enforced emerged from the 'results' book of the other DVU. Entries were analysed for the first six months of 1994 (see Table 4.5). The proportion of cases classified as disputes or 'domestic incidents' ('no crimes'), is lower than in the pre-DVM data (Table 4.1). What has taken their place however is a 'clear up' category, in which the phrase "victim unwilling" repeatedly appears. Whilst in no month (apart from June, but here figures are incomplete) do 'no crimes' exceed 'crimes', between 30–45 per cent of all cases are 'no crimed'.[24] The proportion of cases in which arrests occur and warrants are issued can be calculated either as a proportion of total incidents, or those defined as crimes; giving us approximate figures of 10 per cent and 30 per cent respectively. Here again strong evidence emerged that officers were not arresting where there were grounds to do so.

---

24   A Home Office directive permits 'no-crime' to be a significant clear up category, and it is not seen to reflect on police performance.

Table 4.5 Compiled data from NI domestic violence results book January – June 1994

Month	Incidents	No-crime		Clear-up		Arrest 1		Arrest 2		CW*
		N	%	N	%	N	%	N	%	N
January	96	45	47	41	43	8	8	8	16	2
February	81	37	46	34	42	9	11	9	20	1
March	77	33	43	33	43	8	10	8	18	3
April	79	22	28	49	62	8	10	8	14	-
May**	61	24	39	19	31	7	11	7	19	-
June	125	54	43	20	16	11	9	11	15	4

*   CW means 'circulated on warrant' – this means the perpetrator was not present but an arrest warrant has subsequently been issued.
**   these figures do not add up to the total incidents, since there were blanks in the 'result' column.

The May and June cases were examined in more detail. There were 18 assaults without any result entered, four incidents which were 'no crimed' where offences had occurred (1 criminal damage, two assaults, and one threat). Of the clear ups (where victims were unwilling) 23 were defined as ABH, one as GBH, and two as threats to kill. The small number of 'circulated on warrant', compared to the number of cases where perpetrators are not present, confirms that minimal follow up occurs in this circumstance (an issue raised by a sizeable minority of DVM's users).

The data should not be read as criticisms of the particular DVUs for three reasons. Firstly, two studies (Grace, 1995; Morley and Mullender, 1984) note the difficulties DVU officers have in compiling accurate records, especially in relation to incidence and the outcome of cases. Secondly, the brief of DVUs has been primarily to enhance service to victims of domestic violence, and far less emphasis has been placed upon monitoring and enhancing police response. Thirdly, there is no agreed format for the collection of information either locally, within the Metropolitan Police or nationally.

These difficulties were compounded for DVM, who were reliant on DVUs for data on policing and case outcomes. The DVM database was designed to include information on civil and criminal proceedings, but it proved impossible over the life of the pilot to maintain these aspects with any accuracy; of the 242 incidents on the data base where charges have been entered outcomes were available for 123. The database has been used, however, to track other issues related to law enforcement. An analysis was undertaken to test whether arrests were more likely where the perpetrator and/or victim were from an ethnic minority – the proportions in both cases were slightly lower than in the database sample as a whole. Another analysis was done linking DVM cases where visible injuries were recorded with those where arrests took place. These data are presented in Table 4.6.

The proportion of arrests where visible injuries were present in DVM's case load increased significantly over the pilot. However, when the categories of injury were correlated with arrests it emerged that for almost every category (including knife wounds and broken bones) a higher proportion did not result in arrest than did. Even in cases where there were visible injuries and the perpetrator was present, arrest occurred in only 45 per cent of cases.

Table 4.6 **DVM database correlation between injuries and arrest**

DVM year	Incidents with visible injury	Perp not present		Arrests	
		N	%	N	%
Year 1	123	29	24	34	27
Year 2	236	63	27	76	32
Year 3	159	35	23	67	42

A number of key points can be made from this data:

•   police record keeping – at all levels – is neither systematic nor consistent;

•   even where an offence is recorded by police, arrest and/or charges occur in a minority of incidents;

•   there is a tension in police practice between 'respecting victim's wishes' and law enforcement;

•   the impact of DVM on arrest rates in the borough was not as significant as hoped for.

Case tracking through to prosecution

The lack of reliable data to assess law enforcement responses resulted in an addition to the evaluation; to track a sample of cases involving arrests on DVM's data base through police custody logs, crime desk records and CPS files. Agreement was forthcoming from the police side in terms of access to records and initially from the CPS. In the case of the latter, however, the access was subsequently referred up to regional and national levels resulting in considerable delay. This also meant that the identification of cases had to be re-done, since by the time permission was finally granted many of the files relating to the initial listing of cases were no longer accessible (CPS files are only accessible for 12 months).

The process of laying charges involves the police sending formal notification and documentation through to the CPS. This will include police recommendations regarding whether the defendant should be remanded in custody, or whether bail conditions should be requested. CPS lawyers then have to evaluate the evidence, decide whether the charge is the appropriate one, alter it if they think not, and decide what conditions they will request on the first court appearance. Subsequently, they may request additional evidence be collected by the police, and/or that the police check the willingness of victim/witnesses to proceed. If the victim no longer wishes to continue with the case an official withdrawal statement is needed by the CPS before the file can be closed; police officers take withdrawal statements. CPS lawyers do not meet with victim/witnesses before court appearances to discuss the evidence; this is currently not permitted in England and Wales, although in Scotland procurator fiscals are allowed to do so. Most other common law legal systems now view such contact with victim/witnesses as vital components of case preparation (see also Chapter One).

Tracking cases proved extremely complex. Generating the listings of cases in which arrest had taken place from the DVM database was the only straightforward element. At each subsequent point cases were lost due to the vagaries of record keeping. One police custody record log was missing, and for those that were available cases could not always be found. There was a less that one in two success rate by the CPS in finding the files for the listed cases. From 149 arrest listings, 72 charge records were found, and the CPS traced 34 files. What this demonstrates is both the difficulty of monitoring cases retrospectively, and the 'attrition' rate where data collection is reliant on the vagaries of record keeping in three different agencies.

Despite these limitations the case tracking did produce some interesting data, which further illuminate the complicated issues involved in promoting law enforcement responses to domestic violence. It should be noted that what follows is based solely on the data in the CPS files and DVM case notes, it was not possible, for a variety of reasons, to interview prosecutors about the individual cases.

The cases and outcomes

A total of 56 charges were made with regard to the 34 defendants. The most frequent charges laid by the police were: ABH – Actual Bodily Harm (14); Common Assault (8); Criminal Damage (7); Threats to kill (5); Affray (5); and Breach of the Peace (4). Eight charges were altered by the CPS, with the most common being ABH reduced to common assault, this happened in 40 per cent of ABH charges.

Demographic data were collected to assess if any factors correlated with prosecution. All perpetrators were men and whilst relationship status at the time of the incident was similar to that in the DVM database, a slightly higher proportion of perpetrators were black or from an ethnic minority group. More significantly over half were unemployed and almost two-thirds (62%) had previous convictions (38% for offences involving violence).

Fourteen cases did not proceed to trial (41%); ten were withdrawn before trial (29%) and four (12%) dismissed since witnesses (usually the victim) did not appear. Of the 20 prosecuted cases, there were 19 guilty pleas and one jury trial in which the defendant was convicted. Sentences are recorded in Table 4.7.

Table 4.7 Sentences for the 20 prosecuted cases

Sentence	Number	Comments
Bind over	9	2 with compensation orders
Conditional discharge	5	3 with compensation orders
Probation	4	1 compensation order plus attendance at a men's programme; 1 fine
Custodial	2	4 years; 27 months.

The withdrawal statements included in some files provide insight into the impossibly complex decisions women frequently face. An Angolan woman said (translated from French):

> *I have five children of my own and altogether nine children live in this house with me, I need therefore to be friendly with my husband.*

[The other four were her husband's dead sister's children].

Another young woman withdrew (there was video evidence of use of knife and witness statements) due to family pressure; although in this case the man in question was still found guilty of affray. There was one rape charge which was dropped when the woman concerned felt unable to proceed because of the potential consequences for their son; although here too an assault on her mother was proceeded with. One woman stated explicitly in her withdrawal statement that she pursued prosecution in order to get the man to leave, which he had now done.

Almost half of the cases involved witnesses other than the women themselves (44%), and in all but one case they were able to give evidence. Conviction was somewhat more likely where there was a witness statement and where injury and or threats had been made to others, since even if the original victim withdrew her statement other charges could be pressed. And in some of these cases it was clear that the CPS had chosen to continue with the prosecution, following their guidelines which state that "discontinuance will only take place when all other options have been considered and found to be inappropriate".

The two cases which resulted in custodial sentences bear further examination. The four-year sentence included charges of ABH for assaulting two police officers, and the defendant had a long history of violence and previous convictions. The other resulted from a case where DVM gave considerable support to the woman who had been harassed by an ex-partner for considerable periods of time. This was the only occasion on which the police took a statement which documented abuse over a period of time, *and* the charges related to incidents over the prior six months. It is not clear why this case was treated so differently, although the availability of other (reliable) witnesses may have been a factor.

Issues of concern

Several disturbing issues emerged from the case files. The current practice in the CPS is for each case to have a 'file owner', who has responsibility to ensure that decisions are taken at the appropriate time. Work on individual cases can be undertaken by anyone in the prosecution team. The fact that many individuals were involved was evident from the varied handwriting in each file. Whilst this way of working may be the most efficient for the CPS, it surely also results in a lack of familiarity with, and continuity within, individual cases, and may be particularly ill-suited to the fine judgements and sensitivities needed in domestic violence cases.

Police requested remand in custody to protect victim/witnesses in 14 cases. An example of the grounds police gave was: "victim fears defendant will – if released – try and persuade her to drop charges by violence...".[25] Remand was granted in only three, with the remaining 11 being granted conditional bail (for four of these breaches are later recorded in the CPS files). We were not able to assess whether the CPS applied for remand in all the cases where the police requested it. What was clear, however, was that whilst the police understood that many women may be pressured or coerced to withdraw their complaints, this was not being reflected in magistrates' decisions. Whilst there is a balancing act to be done between the rights of defendants

---

25   Remand was not granted in this case, and the woman withdrew her statement.

and the rights of victims, this data suggest that either currently defendant's liberty is valued more highly than victim's safety by the courts or magistrates simply do not understand the particular circumstances in domestic violence cases.

Although a minority, there were a significant number of files in which CPS lawyers expressed explicit views that withdrawal was expected. For example:

> ... *suggest trial date fixed no sooner than 3 weeks - a domestic relationship between victim and defendant, strong possibility former no longer willing to proceed.*

The first court date was five weeks later and the victim did not appear, she did however inform the court that her child was ill and that she wanted to proceed. The next entry in the file is a month later and involves a request from the CPS to the police to obtain a withdrawal statement. There were an additional four requests from the CPS (within days of getting files) asking the police to confirm that the victim wished to proceed. In two of these cases breaches of bail conditions were reported but not acted upon by the police; both these women withdrew. In the one case which proceeded, it was clear from the DVM files that it was their support which prevented the woman withdrawing. This woman had been upset by what she interpreted as a suggestion from the police that she might want to withdraw, and it was only after a long discussion with a DVM support worker that she decided to proceed. The defendant pleaded guilty.

Whilst understanding the need for the CPS to check whether cases are going to proceed, how they - together with the police - manage this, will communicate subtle messages to women. If there is an expectation of withdrawal within the CPS, and this is communicated implicitly or explicitly to police officers, the danger is that police approaches to the woman will not be an encouraging or supportive one. This is likely to feed into her ambivalence about prosecution, rather than back up her initial resolve to press charges.

There were many examples of breaches of bail conditions in the files, but action was only taken in two cases; both of which eventually resulted in successful prosecutions for the initial charges. This illustrates the importance of swift action where bail is breached to ensure that victim/witnesses are - and feel themselves to be - protected. Whilst action on breach of bail is the responsibility of the police, the CPS also has an interest here since it involves interference with a witness. Whilst limited, these data suggest that where action is taken this supports victim/witnesses in continuing with prosecutions.

In four files, letters were found from the defendants' solicitors stating that they believed the woman wanted to withdraw her statement. One of these cases eventually resulted in conviction, since there were admissions in the man's original statement. All four women did however withdraw their statements. All of these defendants had 'no contact' bail orders, so how were they able to know that women were intending to withdraw without breaking these conditions? Was there not a strong possibility that the woman had been pressured to drop the charges? However, there was no indication in either the CPS files or the DVM documentation that any investigation into potential breaches of bail were requested or undertaken. Rather all that appears in the CPS files are requests to the police asking for a withdrawal statement.

Three men had been on various men's programmes before the recent incident, clearly failing to halt their violence. One was required to attend a programme as part of sentence, and an additional man had referred himself as part of an agreement with the woman to withdraw her statement.

In a review of international research on prosecution (Ford and Regoli, 1993) similar points were made:

> *Generally women hope to secure arrangements enabling them to free themselves from further victimisation. But typically, prosecutors make no effort to understand the victim's situation as a whole, nor do they provide the time and resources necessary to enhance the co-operation and commitment of victims.* (p137–8)

These conclusions are also supported by a very recent report from Victim Support on women's experiences of reporting rape (Victim Support, 1996), and in an Irish report on the needs and experiences of women and children reporting crimes of sexual and physical violence (Working Party on the Legal and Judicial Process, 1996).

Several key points emerge from the data presented in this section:

- there is a failure throughout the criminal justice system to prioritise the safety of victims (by not using remand in custody or pursuing breaches of bail vigorously) which is the foundation on which victims are able to continue with prosecutions;

- the current orientation in the CPS is not one which enables and encourages victim witnesses, and some individuals are clearly still operating from a presumption that women will withdraw;

- where women are enabled to pursue prosecution conviction is likely, most commonly through a guilty plea.

The experience from Canada (see Chapter One) and other jurisdictions (Dobash and Dobash, 1992) suggests that one way of addressing these issues is the creation of trained prosecutors who specialise in domestic violence cases. In some jurisdictions this has been extended to dedicated magistrates and judges, and even the creation of domestic violence courts.[26]

The next section draws on the evaluation questionnaires completed by DVM's users to illuminate what women want from the criminal justice system.

DVM users' assessment of police response and the criminal justice system

Women's experience of policing and law enforcement is explored through the responses of the 223 DVM users who completed the evaluation questionnaires. Forty per cent had called the police previously; 28 per cent on one occasion, 45 per cent on several occasions and 20 per cent many times. Over half were happy with previous police actions, with just under a third reporting variable responses and 16 per cent that they were never happy.

> *I felt safe knowing the police had taken him and I could sleep that night knowing he couldn't come back.*

There were four main complaints: not responding seriously/sympathetically, treating the incident as a 'domestic' (31); failure to arrest or caution (22); response times of 40 minutes or longer (6); no follow-up contact/action when this was promised (6). One woman said:

> *They did not on any other occasion take the assault seriously and usually left without any action which then led to more attacks as he knew the police would do nothing.*

This woman had had two miscarriages and experienced more than 60 assaults. Her recent experience involved driving into the police station car park as she was being chased. Whilst an assault was prevented by her strategy of using the police station, she still had to wait 45 minutes before she was seen by someone.

Sixty-one women reported previous arrests of their partners, including 43 charges and 27 convictions. Two-thirds of sentences comprised a bind over or fine. This group were evenly split on whether action by the criminal justice system had limited the man's violence, although the percentage

---

26   An evaluation of the first year of the Winnipeg Family violence court (Ursel, no date) concludes that "specialization has had a dramatic impact on court outcomes" (pix).

thinking action was effective rose to 80 per cent for the final group of questionnaires. The most frequent reason given by women for intervention having no impact was that the man in question had 'no regard for the law'. Criminal justice intervention has other equally important impacts; two-thirds of women said it made a difference to *them* either because intervention made them feel stronger and supported, or the lack of action increased their sense of hopelessness and being trapped.

Opinion was also divided on the impact of injunctions, with a minority of women before and after contact with DVM seeing them as effective and protective, and the majority reporting that injunctions had been broken, and that there had been minimal, if any, consequences for breaking the order (see also Barron, 1990).

A section of the questionnaire dealt specifically with the recent incident. The majority of contacts with the police were made by women themselves (54%) with children and neighbours accounting for a further 14 per cent. Just under half reported a prompt police response (within a few minutes), a further 27 per cent had to wait 10–20 minutes; and 11 per cent more than 20 minutes. For 7 per cent the police took over an hour to arrive and one woman reported that they never came at all.[27] Delayed response increased over the pilot (the most recent cases record 33% arrival within a few minutes compared to 49% for the first hundred), and suggests that there may have been some effects of sectorisation on response time. Unsurprisingly those who had long waits were amongst the most dissatisfied.

What over two-thirds wanted from the police was for the perpetrator to be arrested/removed, a further quarter wanted them to stop the abuse and/or warn their abuser. A minority wanted escorting to safety. These are somewhat different responses to those in Jane Mooney's Islington survey (1994), in which stopping the violence and getting the man to change were by far the most common responses. This suggests that context affects respondents in research; that referring to a hypothetical situation or an actual (and recent) event produces different responses to a similar question. What most women want when police arrive is some kind of unequivocal intervention.

Women were asked to check off a series of possible actions, drawn from divisional policy and Metropolitan Police guidelines, which the police might have taken. Table 4.8 records their responses; the third column records the percentage reporting these actions in the two interim evaluation reports, comparing these to the final figure gives a sense of change over the course of the pilot. The most marked changes occurred between the first and

---

27   In terms of police procedures the CAD message could not be closed until this call had been responded to. It has been suggested that in this case perhaps what occurred was that the police responded but could not find the woman.

second year of DVM; the most significant being the continued rise in talking with victims alone. These data, when linked to a similar series from police officers (see Table 4.16) demonstrate that elements of what has been considered best practice for a number of years has still not become routine.

Table 4.8   Victims reports of initial police actions in rank order*

Possible actions	Police action		Previous
	N	%**	percentage***
Talk to victim alone	145	90	(65, 75)
Ask if want to talk to DVM	105	65	(65, 56)
Ask if want to press charges	79	49	(49, 44)
Information about injunctions	69	43	(43, 24)
Check if children are present	53	33	(33, 38)
Information about refuges	45	28	(28, 18)
Ask perpetrator to leave	44	27	(27, 24)
Give own name and contact no.	40	25	(25, 24)
Arrest perpetrator	39	24	(24, 27)
Information on other agencies	23	14	(14, 9)
Offer to take to safe place	22	14	(14, 15)
Give written information	19	12	(12, 12)
Talk to victim and perpetrator together	18	11	(11, 3)
Offer to accompany to hospital	8	5	(5, 6)
Phone DVM without consultation	7	4	(4, 6)

*   Rank order means the table is laid out with the most commonly reported actions first.
**   Calculated on base of 160 women where the police were called out.
*** Percentages from interim evaluation reports, calculated on numbers at that stage where police had been called out, with the second year percentage first and first year last.

Most women reported police response as supportive and sympathetic, and that is a change from earlier studies. A significant minority (42), however, were very unhappy with their treatment. Three key complaints emerged: being made to feel they were wasting police time (23); police were hostile, late or did not arrive at all (9); and serious violence – including one incident with a gun – being minimised (8). In response to a question on what else they would have wanted the police to do, by far the majority wanted additional law enforcement and/or protective actions, but a third also referred to the attitude of officers. It is both **what** police do and **how** they do it that matters to women. Police can be sympathetic, yet fail to take action and vice versa. Both these elements need to be stressed in police training. What women want is both assertive action, including arrest, and respectful treatment which supports their right to protection under the law.

I thought they would not assist me because they were too busy owing to the time factor on arrival being one hour from being called out.

They were good but I thought they might have stayed in my flat whilst I got some of my clothes. They told me they were very busy.

They were exceptionally kind and understanding.

They were very matter of fact, I was very distraught and they hassled me with paragraphs when all I wanted was to be safe. I was happy that someone with authority was there as it made my partner come to his senses, but I wasn't happy with how the police handled the situation.

Because it was just me when they arrived, he had gone and got away with what he had done. I would have liked them to arrive promptly after my 999 call.

They blamed me for most of the violence and they didn't realise my injuries were as bad as they were. I had been drinking, I think they knew that and that's why they left me alone, hurt.

My husband pretended nothing had happened and turned it into a comedy, or me being too neurotic. Because the police were all men, they tended to believe him rather than me, even though I had the marks of violence on my hand. They did not take it seriously.

As soon as the police left my husband started it again because he realised that it is impossible to prove. I would have liked them to remove him, or at least tell him that he has no right to throw my things out or threaten me.

The next series of questions were intended to be answered *only* by women who were involved in the prosecution process, and instructions were explicit about this. Many participants where arrest had *not* occurred chose to respond, to take this opportunity to express their opinions about going to court and the legal system. This is but one indication of the strength of feelings which exist about this issue. Responses were analysed for the two distinct groups (see Table 4.9).

Table 4.9   Victims concerns regarding prosecution

Concerns	Arrest		No arrest	
	N	%	N	%
Fear of court appearance	19	25	52	30
Fear of the perpetrator	25	33	63	36
Determined to not let get away with	27	36	43	25
Guilt/disloyalty	4	5	9	5

The data that this 'quirk' produced is extraordinarily revealing, since it shows both similarities and differences between the two groups. Whilst determination not to let the man get away with it is stronger amongst women where arrest has occurred, it is also strong amongst a quarter of women where it did not; these are undoubtedly women who wanted stronger action by the police. The predominant understanding within the criminal justice system is that women's ambivalence about prosecution stems primarily from the context of intimate relationships; but guilt and disloyalty was a residual issue for this group of women. What predominated was fear. Fear in relation to both the perpetrator and the court process. Without provision which addresses these concerns fear and intimidation, rather than guilt and disloyalty, will continue to deter significant numbers of women from pursuing prosecutions.

In the section related to DVM, 28 women reported having fears in relation to the arrest of their partner. By far the most common concern was that it would aggravate the situation, and they might suffer reprisals, especially when release from custody occurred; one commented "He's told me that if I ever called the police he'd kill me". A minority were concerned about what would happen to their partner - whether he'd be hurt, sent to prison, lose his job. The majority (88%) thought that DVM had reassured them - and unsurprisingly this was primarily through having detailed explanations of what would/might happen and what options were open to them immediately, especially applying for an emergency protection order and the possibility of temporary safe accommodation. DVM's availability as backup was also mentioned explicitly by a number of women.

> It's an excellent idea having civilians involved in this area as well as police officers and it's good that I wasn't made to feel I was wasting police time unless I was willing to press charges. The whole thing was taken very seriously and I was not under any pressure to press charges, just given the options and supported either way.

Three women in the follow-up monitoring had been involved in prosecutions, with sentences comprising a bind over for three years, two years probation and a £100 fine. In two cases the woman commented:

The law does not protect the woman or punish the man, it was a very traumatic experience for little result/reward.

I feel very angry because I cannot live at my own home, go to work, go out because he is still able to terrorise me and get away with it.

An additional questionnaire for women withdrawing statements, distributed to both DVUs, IVSS and the local law centre produced only six returns, and none of the women had been referred to DVM. Each woman had particular and specific reasons for withdrawal, but in over half the behaviour of the police was a significant factor. Three women talked of there being an implicit assumption that she would not prosecute.

They asked if I wanted to prosecute, but their attitude was factual, they had no interest in the incident – 'another domestic' attitude. One was looking at his watch and said they couldn't wait long. If I had not been rushed, I may have seen things differently. I had no-one to talk to. It was almost as if the police had decided I wouldn't press charges anyway. They just wanted to get to the next job.

The police were very unhelpful, I would very much have appreciated someone to talk to so I knew what would happen when he got out.

All talked about fear of reprisals if they pursued the case. Each of these women might have benefitted from contact with DVM, and in terms of the local protocol they are precisely the kind of cases DVM was envisaged in relation to. Unfortunately, the reasons why this did not happen are not available to us. They also confirm the importance of *how* police intervene. Communicating disinterest and no confidence in women's ability to see through a prosecution serves to reinforce women's perception that neither they nor domestic violence is taken seriously.

Two questions towards the end of the DVM evaluation questionnaire addressed a law enforcement approach to domestic violence, and whether recent police action would affect their willingness to call the police in future. An overwhelming majority (90%) thought domestic violence should *always* be treated as a crime, with the majority of the remainder opting for the 'sometimes' response; only two (less than 1%) thought it should not. Just under half said that their willingness to call the police had been affected, with virtually all reporting a more positive perception of the police, and an increased willingness to report; much of this was attributed to the presence of DVM locally.

The key points from this data are:

- women want respectful treatment by, and assertive action from the police – but they do not always receive either or both;

- victims of domestic violence think domestic violence should be responded to as a crime, but need support and protection in order for these be a viable option;

- a proportion of police officers communicate that domestic violence is trivial and/or that they do not believe that women will pursue prosecution;

- that where prosecutions do occur, the sentences given are perceived by victims as failing to sanction on men's behaviour.

The questionnaires completed by police officers provide some insight into why police response is inconsistent and why the law enforcement element of DVM's aims was so difficult to achieve.

Police attitudes and responses to domestic violence.

Three questionnaires were completed by police officers in 1993 (Q1), 1994 (Q2) and 1995 (Q3).[28] Following poor response rates using internal mail for the first questionnaire, the second and third were completed in training sessions. Police put most effort into increasing response rates for the second questionnaire, and this is reflected in the comparative returns (Q1-106,[29] Q2-181, Q2-157). The tone of officers' responses changed over the three questionnaires; there was considerable hostility to both DVM and the evaluation expressed in the first, but in the second and third far more practical suggestions for improvements in relationships between victims, police and DVM were evident.

Data have been selected from individual questionnaires and across all three to elucidate the barriers to increasing law enforcement responses to domestic violence.

Over the three questionnaires, officers were evenly split between those who had five years or less employment in the police service and those who had six years or more. The turnover in staff is marked with between 10–15 per centhaving been in the borough for less than a year at the point they completed questionnaires. Men were a majority of respondents (80% plus for each one), and a very small percentage of officers were from ethnic minorities.

---

28   The 1993 questionnaire had two versions – for operational officers and managers, the subsequent two were only for operational officers. All contained a common core of questions, with others being adapted to the phase of DVM at the time and other operational issues, such as sectorisation, the change from DVU to VPU.
29   The 58 managers are not included in this analysis.

Q1 and Q2 explored definitions of domestic violence, since this has a bearing on both record keeping and what actions officers take. In Q1 officers were asked to define domestic violence in an open ended question. Coding was conducted on two components of the definitions – what forms of violence were included and how the relationship/location of the incident was specified. The most common elements in forms of violence were violence and aggression (34%), physical violence and threats (33%), another third of officers however included variations on emotional and verbal abuse, disputes and arguments. The home/family was the most common location specified (32%), followed by partners (25%) and a combination (14%). These components combined in variable ways; from wide and inclusive definitions of both violence and context to much more limited definitions which specified injury and partner relationships. This confusion between what in the literature has been called 'family violence' and the more usual meaning of 'domestic violence' (violence and abuse by current and ex-partners, predominantly by men to women) is also evident in the Metropolitan Police guidelines, which contains a vague and inclusive definition. Whilst there were positive reasons for widening the definition – to ensure the inclusion of all incidents and extend the remit for police intervention – there are also significant drawbacks which turn primarily on impeding the development of a clear and consistent police response, and assessment of police responses.

What became apparent in discussions with officers about the 'crime sheet issue' (see Chapter Six) was that they make distinctions between domestic violence (which they define as crime) and domestic disputes (which they do not). Q2 explored this definitional issue and asked what proportion of cases officers allocated to each category. Over three-quarters of officers (85%) thought there was a difference, and 70 per cent maintained that domestic violence involved the use or threat of violence, whereas a domestic dispute was confined to verbal interchanges and argument. The consensus about what distinguished the two categories was, however, not reflected in allocations of cases they had dealt with in the last year (see Table 4.10).

Table 4.10 Officers' allocation of cases over the past year to domestic dispute or domestic violence

Proportion of cases	Domestic dispute (%)	Domestic violence (%)
Under 20%	9	16
20–39%	10	25
40–59%	24	26
60–79%	24	13
80–100%	15	4
Other responses	18	16

Neither the distribution between the categories nor the proportions allocated within each are uniform. In one sense this lack of consensus is not surprising, definitions are intensely contested in all fields. The range of disagreement is nonetheless disturbing, suggesting that police discretion is informed by differing perceptions of (or ways of investigating) domestic violence, which will inevitably produce variable and inconsistent practice.

In Q1 officers were also asked a series of questions about their knowledge of domestic violence: what proportion of relationships it occurs in, what the primary cause is, the proportion of the victims which are female and the average number of incidents which take place before the police are called. There was no consistency in response to any of these questions, in fact, wide disparities were commonplace. Data are presented here for the gendered distribution of victimisation, since this became an issue of contention between some police officers and DVM (officers defining DVM as biased for referring to victims as women). Officers were asked to estimate the proportion of victims that were female, and at a later point to record the proportion of cases they had dealt with in the last 12 months which involved female victims. Table 4.11 records responses to both these questions. Officers experiential knowledge – three-quarters report that 95 per cent plus of the victims they see are women – is not reflected in their conceptual knowledge where only a third report this estimate. Opinion is a stronger influence than policing realities in constructing beliefs and attitudes.

Table 4.11   Domestic violence and gender

Proportion of victims female	Actual cases* %	Theoretical estimate** %
All	40	2
95%	35	31
90%	14	35
75%	8	20
50%	2	12

*   These were the cases which officers had dealt with in the previous 12 months.
**   This is the proportion of victims officers *think* are female.

This accumulation of data demonstrates that there is currently no shared knowledge base amongst the police about domestic violence. These fundamental issues need to be addressed *in detail* through training. Unless and until this happens women calling the police are entering a lottery, in which one officer will define her experience as a crime, whilst another will not.

The next series of data relate to officers' attitudes and responses to domestic violence in terms of law enforcement. Data from a number of questions show that support for a law enforcement response was fragile, and does not seem to have become more deep rooted over the pilot. Table 4.12 records responses to a series of statements about the policing of domestic violence from each of the three questionnaires (Q1, Q2 and Q3). There are marked inconsistencies between officers and over the three questionnaires, with similar proportions supporting mediation and arrest as the best response; and the proportion supporting the former increased over time whilst the latter decreased. Increasing support for law enforcement over time was, however, evident in responses from NI, where it was less strong at the beginning of the pilot.

Table 4.12 Attitudes to policing of domestic violence*

Statement	Agree			Neutral			Disagree		
	Q1	Q2	Q3	Q1	Q2	Q3	Q1	Q2	Q3
Mediation is the best approach	43	49	56	37	41	34	20	10	10
Police should not intervene in family disputes	9	18	8	16	34	22	75	48	68
Arrest of the perpetrator is the best response	40	35	33	29	37	39	31	28	29
Victim's rights are often ignored by the police	3	8	5	10	19	5	87	83	90
Offender's rights are often ignored by the police	12	13	13	21	16	13	66	70	74
Most women don't mean it when they want arrest	28	26	24	29	36	38	43	38	38
Arrest is a waste a time, women will drop the charges	20	27	24	19	30	24	61	43	52
Arrest is a waste of time, CPS will drop the charges	29	33	20	23	34	37	48	33	42
Domestic violence should be handled as any other assault	63	57	61	11	18	16	26	24	22
Arrest is as likely if the perpetrator is a police officer	61	62	65	26	24	19	13	10	14
Arrest is more likely if the perpetrator is from an ethnic minority	0	3	2	4	11	7	96	83	92
Arrest is less likely if the perpetrator is upper or middle class	11	9	7	8	9	12	81	77	80

*   All figures are percentages

Each questionnaire attempted to tap the factors affecting willingness to arrest. In Q1 officers were asked to rank a series of statements in terms of whether they would increase or decrease the likelihood of arrest. Arrest was considered more likely where the following (in rank order) were present: evidence of injury; officer witnessing the assault; breach of a current court order; willingness of victim to testify. Arrest was deemed less likely (also in rank order) where: the victim used drugs or alcohol; where the perpetrator had a criminal record (although the data from the CPS earlier in this chapter present a different picture); another priority call; previous incidents.

A slightly different approach was used in Q2. Rather than a forced choice format officers were asked to list three factors which increased the likelihood of arrest and three which decreased it. Because there were no standardised answers, the data are complex, and only the most frequently mentioned issues are discussed here. Whilst similar to the rankings in Q1, there are more nuances, and additional issues appear.

In terms of arrest being more likely (see Table 4.13) the 'seriousness' of an assault, strength of evidence, presence of children and preventing further violence feature strongly.

Table 4.13 Factors increasing likelihood of arrest

Factor	Percentage
Serious injuries/assault, strength of evidence	56
Children involved/at risk	37
To prevent breach of the peace/likely further assault	31
Previous violence/repeat attack	24
Victim wishes/willingness to substantiate	24
Injury/an assault has occurred/offence committed	21
Offender violent/threatening in police presence	18
Behaviour/attitude of perpetrator	17
Victim safety/fear of further assault	14
Alcohol/offender unreasonable	11

*   This was an open ended, multiple response question.

Many of the factors influencing officers' decisions are either much broader or narrower than those informing force and divisional policy: i.e. that an arrestable offence has occurred, and/or to prevent a further assault/breach. Four predominate: that there is evidence of a *serious* assault; the behaviour of the offender; the need to protect children; and the wishes of the victim. This supports feedback in briefing meetings by the DVM staff (recorded in several quarterly reports) of officers concerns about 'unwarranted' arrests, and an unwillingness to take a law enforcement position if they *think* the victim will not make a statement/carry the case forward (an attitude noted by a number of DVM users in the previous section).

The factors which officers said were likely to decrease the probability of arrest (Table 4.14) raise even more concerns about current practice, both in their content and their variability between officers. A selection of the more worrying responses were:

Victim known to be unsatisfactory e.g. drunk, wastes police time.

Children are content and well cared for.

The house is clean and respectable.

If I believe victim will drop charges.

First time offender who unlikely to reoffend.

Victim 'gobby'.

Perpetrator resides in the home.

Table 4.14 Factors decreasing likelihood of arrest*

Factor	Percent
Suspect willing to leave/has left	31
Victim refusal/unwillingness to substantiate	30
first incident/violence unlikely to continue	23
Minor injuries/assault, non-visible injuries	17
Victim just want man removed/victim wishes	14
Attitude of victim	14
No violence/offence	13
Prior calls to same address/history of withdrawing complaints	11
All quiet when police arrive	5

*   This was an open ended, multiple response question.

Again what we see are many factors which are irrelevant to whether an arrestable offence has occurred, with officers making distinctions on the 'seriousness' of the assault/offence and how they 'assess' the individuals involved. It is also interesting to note that similar factors appear in both lists (the presence of children, repeat calls to the same address) meaning that the same information denotes opposite actions for different officers. Whilst for some officers a history of abuse is a factor which makes arrest more likely and more desirable, for others they are both less likely to arrest and less sympathetic. Here a pathologising of the victim replaces responding on the evidential grounds which police officers maintain they work from. This needs to be addressed by police managers and the possibility raised that part of the problem might be previous responses by agencies; that from the police perspective it may be that what is needed is a *stronger* rather than a weaker law enforcement response.

Value judgements about the woman whether she is a 'deserving victim' are evident, as are stereotypes about the home and care of children being indicators of the content of the relationships concerned. The misinterpretation of coping strategies noted in Chapter Three is evident in these responses. The relevance of 'value judgements' to officers' actions was confirmed in responses to a later question which asked for a description of the last domestic violence call the respondent attended. In many of the cases where arrest occurred, continued aggression which the police were either witness to, or the recipients of, was noted; and in many where arrest did not occur negative assessments of, or remarks about, the victim were made. Another common theme between these questions was officers use of the term 'minor assault', and the implication that this was not therefore a law enforcement matter, which by Q3 had become 'common assault' following recent policy changes regarding charging standards and case disposal (see Chapter Six).

Making immediate assessments and judgements are an essential element in police work, but they are clearly being based on officers' own values, rather than either the 'facts of the case' or what we know about domestic violence. One example of these processes at work are the substantial number of responses which refer to incidents being 'a one off', violence as unlikely to re-occur. This is an interpretation, and contrasts with many studies which show police are seldom called to first assaults, and that violence tends to be repeated.

Officers' attitudes to positive arrest policies were canvassed across the three questionnaires, and data appears in Table 4.15. Whilst this data could be interpreted as supporting a positive arrest approach, since the majority at each point saw it as protecting victims and promoting important messages to communities, there was less agreement on whether it would act as a deterrent, or encourage prosecution and uncertainty about the effects in terms of willingness to call the police or the dangerousness of perpetrators. Shifts (albeit relatively small) over time are in the direction noted elsewhere: away from stronger support for pro-law enforcement responses and towards equivocation. This uncertainty is to some extent reflected in the findings from a number of studies in the US on mandatory arrest (see Dobash and Dobash, 1992). But in a recent review of the methodology and findings in these studies Zorza (1995) concludes that no other police action is more effective as a deterrent.

Table 4.15   Police perceptions of positive arrest policies*

Views on positive arrest	Agree			Unsure			Disagree		
	Q1	*Q2*	*Q3*	*Q1*	*Q2*	*Q3*	*Q1*	*Q2*	*Q3*
Protects victims of abuse	60	43	44	18	39	32	22	17	23
Prevents future violence	30	19	16	24	35	38	46	45	45
Promotes an important message to the community	69	49	58	23	36	24	8	15	18
Increases willingness of victims to follow through prosecution if police lay the charge	35	28	29	24	29	25	41	43	44
Makes victims less willing to call the police	12	17	16	48	45	43	40	36	41
Will make perpetrators more dangerous	13	19	9	40	42	43	47	39	48
Reduces police discretion	53	59	57	18	24	19	28	15	24

*   All figures are percentages

Responses to questions about why victims call the police and why they might withdraw complaints also highlighted stark differences between officers, with a section responding in thoughtful and perceptive ways and others with unreflective cynicism. But even those who were thoughtful took contradictory positions; recognising the ways women are intimidated by their abusers and the justice system whilst positing 'victim wishes' as uncomplicated.

A series of questions based on divisional and Metropolitan Police policy and practice guidelines in relation to domestic violence was compiled. Responses are presented in Table 4.16.

Table 4.16 Police officers' responses to domestic violence calls in relation to force and local policy*

Possible actions	Always			Sometimes			Never		
	Q1	Q2	Q3	Q1	Q2	Q3	Q1	Q2	Q3
Talk with victim alone	87	80	80	13	19	20	-	1	-
Talk with victim and perpetrator together	17	11	12	72	75	73	11	13	15
Check if children witnessed	50	60	46	47	38	52	3	2	2
Tell victim about refuges/safe housing	37	35	40	62	64	59	1	1	1
Discuss pressing charges	74	62	67	26	38	38	-	-	-
Advise victim on other legal remedies (injunctions etc.)	73	75	69	26	24	30	1	1	1
Provide written information**	14	-	-	66	-	-	20	-	-
Provide victim with DVM referral card**	-	29	37	--	52	55	-	19	7
Provide victim with officer name, number, station phone number	33	28	24	54	56	66	13	16	9
Offer to take victim to place of safety	20	12	19	76	81	77	4	7	4
Ask perpetrator to leave	10	6	7	87	93	91	3	1	2
Caution perpetrator	10	9	1	79	76	73	11	14	25
Arrest perpetrator	5	1	5	95	99	95	--	-	-
Refer case to DVM**	-	46	49	-	51	49	-	2	2
Refer case to police DVU	82	56	58	18	43	41	-	1	1
Refer case to VSS	23	15	11	64	64	73	13	20	16

*   All figures are percentages
**   First questionnaire only
*** Second and third questionnaires

A number of the key elements of what are considered current best practice (such as providing information about refuges and the officers' name and contact number) are still not integrated into daily practice. Of particular concern are the officers who say they 'never' act in ways which force and divisional guidelines recommend, and the fact that only a third routinely gave out the DVM referral card. The quotes which follow illustrate both resistance to, and support for, the law enforcement principle embodied in DVM.

I don't care what service policy is, it is up to the officer that attends the scene whether to arrest or not.

Too much time is spent on these incidents to the detriment of others when there clearly is going to be no further action.

Just because there are grounds for arrest it is not always wise to use this power, it should be used with discretion.

I'm too busy dealing with other things.

Breach of the Peace cost in overtime – this is sometimes a consideration.

I think police willingness has increased since DVM began, not just in the last six months.

DVM has made some police officers realise that domestic violence is a crime.

Officers were asked to record the number of arrests for domestic violence they had made in the previous 12 months, and then to estimate the proportion this represented of calls they attended (see Table 4.17).

Table 4.17 Police officers' reports of number and proportion of arrests during the DVM pilot

Arrests in last year	Q1	Q2	Q3	Proportion of cases where arrest	Q1	Q2	Q3
None	32	21	39	Less than 10%	47	41	33
1–4	55	51	49	11–25%	30	31	27
5–10	10	21	9	26–40%	5	14	14
11–20	2	2	3	41–60%	8	7	10
21–30	–	1	–	61–80%	7	4	8
Don't know	–	3	4	more than 80%	3	2	2

*   All figures percentages

Clearly arrest is not used in the majority of domestic violence calls. Some of this may be attributable to the limitations on police action – that the incident in question did not involve a crime, or even if it did constitute a crime, it was not an arrestable offence.[30] However, the range of responses from

---

30   Police officers also have powers to make preventative arrests under PACE (1984) where they have concerns about risk of assault to a vulnerable person. This power was one of those listed on the DVM 'aide memoire'.

officers in response to these questions cannot be so easily explained away; it is unlikely that those who have made many arrests just happened to be called to incidents where arrestable offences had occurred. The fact that arrest is not used in many cases contrasts somewhat with the opinion expressed in a later question in which almost half of officers believed that the willingness to arrest had increased, primarily because of increased awareness and changes in police policy. It is this lack of correspondence between what officers *think* is happening generally and what they report *doing* personally which makes the accurate collection and regular collation of data essential; otherwise there is no basis on which to distinguish between rhetoric and reality.

Explaining the limited movement in relation to law enforcement

Several structural issues made the achievement of enhanced law enforcement responses much more difficult than establishing crisis intervention. Working across two divisions, which had different styles of management (and in one division four different chief superintendents during the three year pilot) were potent stumbling blocks to creating common practice.

A small team of civilians have neither the resources nor power to create extensive change in police policy or practice. What should not be forgotten, however, is that DVM substantially enhanced the opinion of the police amongst victims, and probably encouraged reporting of subsequent incidents. The primary responsibility for 'delivering' the law enforcement element of DVM's aims lay with the police themselves, who were co-sponsors of the pilot. The management of the pilot also bear some responsibility for making the police in the two divisions accountable. A number of recommendations were made in interim evaluation reports to address the problem, very few of which were fully implemented.

The training of officers planned for the initial phase was reduced in length and scope, and subsequent calls for training were not implemented at all in one division, and only comprised one hour dealing with a case study in the other. Attempts to develop common record keeping systems and address the complex issues involved in relation to completion of crime sheets was never adequately resolved. The suggestion, arising from the Canada study trip, that a senior officer in both divisions be appointed to monitor police responses, to ensure consistency, adherence to law enforcement policies (offering 'spot' advice and training to individual officers where policy has not been followed), was reduced to a single month's monitoring of calls and responses.

That said, however, the issues extend far beyond this particular area, to policing of domestic violence generally. Whilst both the limitations of the data available, and its content, are somewhat disappointing in relation to law enforcement responses, data collected on the DVM study trip to Canada demonstrated that such problems are still in evidence even where concerted efforts have occurred at local, state and federal levels for over ten years. No doubt similar inconsistencies would be found in any British police division subjected to intense scrutiny (see also Grace, 1995; Wright, 1995).

What DVM has shown, however, are the potentials where certain elements can be combined. There are a number of cases which exemplify this, where DVM was contacted early on and able to provide the kind of support that makes a difference to women, even where initial police actions were not as strong as they could have been. One of DVM's support workers provided this example of when the crisis intervention and law enforcement elements combined as originally envisaged.

> *This is a black woman, she's a teacher in a local school and her boyfriend's white. He'd been harassing her for quite some time. She came in and I spent quite a bit of time with her and advised her to get an injunction. She didn't want to do anything with the police initially, she didn't have much faith in the way the police responded the times she'd called them out. She got an injunction and she had to call the police again and they dealt with it. She felt because he was white they said 'look he just wants to talk to you, why don't you sit down together and have a chat' but they did suggest contacting us. We talked over what had happened, he was clearly in breach of an injunction. I took it up and got the DVU involved who followed it through, including I think talking to the officers involved. It all started to be taken seriously and the net result was he was arrested and last Friday he was sentenced to two years and three months, for two threats to kill and common assault. That's a perfect example of how DVM actually co-ordinated something. (SW4)*

Comments from the clerk at the magistrates court confirm that DVM has had an influence with respect to prosecutions.

> *We see more cases than we have ever done, an increase in the number of common assault cases prosecuted. DVM has meant that women are more willing to give evidence, having the court procedure explained calms their fears. (Magistrates' Court Clerk)*

Whilst the DVM study visit to Canada made clear that movement to law enforcement responses to domestic violence is painstakingly slow, minimal change occurs without consistent and strong support from government, senior management, reinforcement through training and sanctions for failure to implement policy.

Implications for policy and practice

In this concluding section the evaluation findings which have implications for future policy and practice development in the criminal justice system have been compiled. The majority refer to police practice, primarily because more evidence was generated by the pilot and evaluation on this issue. Both the limited number of cases proceeding to prosecution, and the 'attrition' in tracking these cases meant that data relating to the CPS, courts and probation were far more limited. Whilst these points rely on data from a particular area, and in relation to a specific project, the issues raised extend to the policing and prosecution of domestic violence throughout the UK, and beyond. This section should be read in conjunction with the overall conclusions and recommendations in Chapter Seven.

- Over two-thirds of women wanted the police to arrest or remove the perpetrator, a further quarter wanted them to stop the abuse and/or warn their abuser.

- Victims of domestic violence think domestic violence should be responded to as a crime, but need support and protection in order for these be a viable option.

- Both *what* police do and *how* they do it matters to women. Police can be sympathetic, yet fail to take action and vice versa; and on occasion neither is forthcoming. Both these elements need to be stressed in police training. What women want is both assertive action, including arrest, and respectful treatment which supports their right to protection under the law.

- A proportion of police officers communicate that domestic violence is trivial and/or that they do not believe that women will pursue prosecution.

- Data from police officers and women who had called the police confirmed that elements of what has been considered best practice for a number of years has still not become routine.

- Even where an offence is recorded by police, arrest and/or charges occur in a minority of incidents.

- There is a tension in police practice between 'respecting victim's wishes' and law enforcement.

- Different officers view the same factors as making an arrest more or less likely (the presence of children, repeat calls to the same address); thus the same information denotes opposite actions.

- Where repeat calls are known about a proportion of officers respond by pathologising the victim, rather than investigating the specific complaint. This needs to be addressed by police managers and the possibility raised that part of the problem might be previous responses by agencies; that from the police perspective it may be that what is needed is a *stronger* rather than weaker law enforcement response.

- Officers justify not using law enforcement responses by referring to incidents as 'a one off', that violence is unlikely to re-occur. This is an interpretation, and contrasts with many studies which show police are seldom called to first assaults, and that violence tends to be repeated.

- In a significant proportion of calls (a third upwards) by the time the police arrive the perpetrator is no longer there; minimal action is subsequently taken in the vast majority of such cases, despite circular 60/1990 stressing the 'apprehension of offenders'.

- Police record keeping – at all levels – is neither systematic nor consistent.

- Data on the *actual* gender of victims, combined with what police *think* the gendered distribution of victimisation is, revealed that opinion is a stronger influence than policing realities in constructing beliefs and attitudes.

- There is a disturbing lack of correspondence between what officers *think* is happening generally and what they report *doing* personally which makes the accurate collection and regular collation of data essential; otherwise there is no basis on which to distinguish between rhetoric and reality.

- There is currently no shared knowledge base amongst the police about domestic violence. These fundamental issues need to be addressed in *detail* through training. Unless and until this happens women calling the police are entering a lottery, in which one officer will define her experience as a crime, whilst another will not.

- Tracking cases through the legal process retrospectively, resulted in a substantial 'attrition' rate due to the vagaries of record keeping in different agencies.

- There is a failure throughout the criminal justice system to prioritise the safety of victims (by not using remand in custody or pursuing breaches of bail vigorously) which is the foundation on which victims are able to continue with prosecutions.

- The current orientation in the CPS is not one which enables and encourages victim witnesses, and some individuals are clearly still operating from a presumption that women will withdraw.

- Where women are enabled to pursue prosecution conviction is likely, most commonly through a guilty plea.

5 Inter-agency links and co-ordination

The third element of DVM's aims was to improve inter-agency co-ordination, promote consistent practice within the borough, and highlight gaps in service provision. Here data from phased surveys of local agencies, the questionnaires to DVM users and interviews with DVM staff are used to explore this element of DVM's work. There are a number of ways in which inter-agency links developed; through formal and informal networking during DVMPMG meetings and other local fora; through the daily practice of crisis intervention; through the potentials which particular times and places create; and through planned strategic intervention. The majority of DVM's work and influence occurred through the first three possibilities, partly because the PMG failed to fulfil its envisaged role (see Chapter Six), and partly as this chapter will demonstrate because there were unanticipated outcomes from the daily practice of crisis intervention. The other successful element in the inter-agency work was the evolution of strong working links between DVM and the LADVC.

Before exploring the research data, however, some further discussion, complementing that in Chapter Six, on the role and activity of the PMG is needed. The PMG was envisaged as having the primary role in developing the inter-agency aspect of DVM's aims; Chapter Six explores why it did not formally fulfil this, or any of its other designated responsibilities in the ways that were envisaged. Some of the possible reasons were: variable membership and attendance; the spill over of rivalry and dissension from other parts of DVMs structure; and that recruitment had not targeted the most appropriate membership. There are, however, a number of other possible factors involved.

There was both a lack of clarity about the precise place of the PMG in the structure of DVM – did it have autonomy to make decisions about policy and practice, or did these have to always be referred back to the EG? This was never explicitly addressed, and almost by default policy documents from the PMG were referred through to the EG. Issues about formal power were involved, but the PMG as a body chose never to question, contest or raise this matter formally. There was potential to have considerably more influence, but this was not grasped (or maybe even not understood) by the PMG.

It is also arguable that the expectations of the PMG were too far-reaching from the outset, since it was charged with a number of crucially important tasks: creating policy and practice for DVM; being the mechanism through which change in the criminal justice system was to be effected; developing the inter-agency aim of DVM. Even the latter aspect had a number of elements to it, including: establishing a consensus locally that domestic violence was, and should be responded as a crime; building linked and consistent responses across the borough; and acting as a bridge between DVM and other agencies in terms of crisis intervention. These are substantial responsibilities for a group of people who had extensive responsibilities in their own agencies, often only a part of which involved domestic violence. On reflection perhaps if these tasks had been prioritised, and work planned over the lifetime of the pilot several, if not all, of the areas might have been given detailed attention.

Whilst the PMG undoubtedly did not fulfil the intentions and hopes invested in it, there were a number of ways in which DVM contributed to inter-agency development in the borough.

The local context at the outset, and first phase of DVM

The first two phased questionnaires to agencies in the borough were themselves an instance of partnership, being designed to combine evaluation requirements and the information needs of the Local Authority Domestic Violence Co-ordinator (LADVC); mapping the current levels of awareness, training needs and gaps in provision were shared concerns. Distribution was divided between the two, although all the analysis was undertaken by the evaluator.[31]

The data from these questionnaires are unlike that from the police and service users, since those completing it were doing so on behalf of an organisation – an inherently problematic exercise. One person was required to complete the questionnaire from the perspective of the agency rather than their own experience, attitudes or practice. It is, however, the only way of approximating agency practice across a wide range of organisations and groups where time and resources are limited.

The first phase questionnaire was distributed to just under 350 statutory and voluntary sector groups/agencies, with specific targeting of organisations working with Black and ethnic minority groups, the elderly, people with disabilities and lesbians and gay men. The return rate was just over 25 per cent for both groupings (once the inaccuracy of the voluntary sector listings was taken into account). A total of 85 were returned (56 from statutory, 29

---

31   With colleagues in the Child and Woman Abuse Studies Unit.

from the voluntary sector). The low response rate from the statutory sector is in part due to the fact that distribution unfortunately coincided with a lengthy strike and policy of non-co-operation with the local authority. Responses from the voluntary sector groups were more varied, since they ranged from groups specialising in support for women experiencing domestic violence to groups whose contact with domestic violence was minimal. A number of organisations returned questionnaires without completing them, with notes saying that the issue was not relevant to them, which may account for the low response rate from the voluntary sector.

Of those returning completed questionnaires, only a minority reported that they could not/did not support women, and this was usually because their role precluded direct service provision. It was also a minority which provided focused services in relation to domestic violence, with the majority seeing their role as referring on; primarily to refuges/Women's Aid, police DVUs; local law centres and solicitors. This confirms the point made in Chapter Three; that agency interventions tend to focus on ending the relationship/violence.

Very few groups (just under a third) kept records of domestic violence cases; analysis of the numbers estimated for the last month revealed that (even without the local refuges) substantially more enquiries per group were made to voluntary sector groups, highlighting the importance of the direct support services they provide and that the voluntary sector is a vital intermediary point between individuals and statutory services.

A small minority had written policy on domestic violence, this was more common in the statutory sector. The knowledge base on domestic violence, housing rights and legal issues, whilst somewhat stronger in the statutory sector, was overall quite weak. This is somewhat concerning since women contact agencies expecting that they will be able to provide accurate advice and information.

A series of questions probed how women with additional needs were responded to. Responses revealed a defensiveness around 'equal opportunities issues'. The questions were either read by respondents, or the issues understood, as suggesting they 'discriminated' in their service provision, rather than as an enquiry into what additional awareness and forms of support might be necessary/offered. Most groups had been contacted by a range of women, the least common being contact by lesbians. Very few had had more than the occasional (if that) enquiry from a man being victimised in either a heterosexual or homosexual relationship. This data raised issues relating to gaps in services for particular groups of women which were subsequently taken up by the LADVC, who conducted more focused surveys and developmental work on services for Black and ethnic minority women and disabled women.

Over two-thirds of respondents wanted to offer more support for those experiencing domestic violence. The most commonly mentioned factors which would enable this were: better referral information (15); specialist training (13); more resources (11). Only 20 per cent of the statutory agencies and even less in the voluntary sector had had training on domestic violence; this prompted a recommendation that the local authority training programme be opened up to the voluntary sector.

Data from this questionnaire were used by both DVM and the LADVC to: produce referral directories; develop networking and training; highlight potential members of DVM Programme Management Group; extend contacts for publicity/information distribution; and point up areas needing further attention. The extent of interest amongst agencies in developing awareness and skills was used by the LADVC to plan subsequent work. A number of the gaps in awareness, knowledge and provision which this first survey raised were addressed by the LADVC, the kind of collaborative work which was envisaged when the post was first created.

Following the first interim evaluation report discussions took place with the LADVC about how her work and that of DVM could be complementary rather than overlapping. Especially important was potential duplication between DVMPMG and the local authority co-ordinated domestic violence forum. The different priorities for areas of work was seen to preclude overlap, with the exception of work on legal issues which it was agreed to pursue through a combining of the forum and DVMPMG sub-groups. However no-one from the local authority group ever attended the legal sub-group, apart from the LADVC herself on one occasion.

Building links

During the first 18 months of the pilot the staff team became more knowledgeable about the other agencies in the borough, and particular contacts and working relationships developed. What emerged initially was a similar variability in response to that encountered in the police. The co-ordinator noted in an early quarterly report:

> *Not only is there not a proper policy on homelessness regarding domestic violence, but in every single neighbourhood office there are different policies and practices, and each individual does it differently.*

Extensive liaison with the LADVC emerged, through which poor practice could be highlighted, and where necessary additional pressure put on particular agencies in relation to particular cases and more generally. Feedback from DVM was used to sustain pressure by the LADVC for implementation of the local good practice guidelines which she had written, and for priority to be given to training on them across and between agencies.

The detailed knowledge built through daily practice enabled the support workers to become skilled advocates for women. DVM was also able to develop particular links to enhance local service provision, especially at this point in terms of the provision of legal services and advice.

The second phase agency questionnaire was designed to assess awareness of DVM locally, and the impact of some of the LADVC's developmental work. A poor response rate to this survey (only 30 were returned, although the sample base was smaller as mailing lists were updated to remove non-existent groups and those which reported no contact with domestic violence in the first questionnaire) was possibly the result of the number of questionnaires on domestic violence distributed in the borough during 1994.[32] Most of the agencies responding were aware of DVM, and many had direct contact. It was seen as an important additional asset in local provision.

Both the DVM data base and users' evaluation questionnaires demonstrate the range of referrals made by DVM. By the end of the pilot 90 different local agencies/organisations had been used. The majority of DVM users did not know about either the agency at all, or that they could get support/assistance from them in relation to domestic violence. DVM was, therefore, effective in both discovering local support resources and in informing women about them.

The impact of the DVM pilot

The final phase survey of agencies was done by telephone to increase response rates, and the 30 agencies which DVM had most contact with comprised the sample: 24 were interviewed (14 statutory services and 10 voluntary sector). This interview was primarily orientated to assessing the impact of DVM locally.

By this stage in the pilot contacts between DVM and other agencies had shifted from DVM being the primary referring and contact agency to a much more reciprocal liaison; each referring to the other and seeking advice or information in relation to particular cases.

Over two-thirds of groups thought DVM had made a difference to their work on domestic violence (and a slightly higher number thought DVM had made a difference for victims of domestic violence). Those which had most

---

32   At least two had been done by the LADVC

contact were much more likely to report effects on their practice. DVM's role and skill as advocates was confirmed by several agencies who provided both emergency services and more long term support.

They chase us up when we are busy and can't respond fast enough – they very positively chase us. (LBI Emergency Lock Service)

The importance of DVM in both co-ordinating responses (one element in the inter-agency aim), and establishing important groundwork so that referrals were appropriate was also a common theme. Whilst it is impossible to separate out the impact of DVM and the work of the LADVC in raising the issue of domestic violence locally, the quotes which follow refer to the direct contact agencies had with DVM.

It hasn't changed our policies, but has affected our attitudes, and encouraged a more co-ordinated approach and liaison. (LBI Housing Officer)

It is valuable helping women to access our services and they provide support if they have to wait a few weeks for an appointment. (Women's Counselling Project)

Someone is always there, so we can build up working relationships. We are confident that they know what they are doing, refer appropriately unlike the DVUs. (Solicitor)

In homelessness work it has helped to deal quickly and sympathetically with cases, because they are a point of reference. Women have said that they found it very helpful. (LBI Homelessness Officer)

I get all my injunction work from DVM and DVUs, and do about five emergency applications a week. Women would not get those injunctions otherwise, they don't respond to advertising, they only seek injunctions following being given personal advice. (Solicitor)

The particular importance of DVM locally was attributed to their availability out of hours, their role as advocates for women, and the linking and co-ordination role they performed.

We hear very positive reports from women, different from the DVUs, much more helpful. (Women's Counselling Project)

They are incredibly good, it's never difficult to get through, we wouldn't want to lose them. (LBI Social Worker)

They work long hours and at weekends, and can drop everything to go out to a woman. Their whole expertise is domestic violence. We have women speaking very highly of them when they are referred to us for longer term work. (IVSS)

It enables women to get a better and more personal service from other agencies; that they make the referral means women are less nervous. (LBI Homelessness Officer)

Women can have a supported journey through the many and varied agencies, someone with them easing the way. Having someone there providing ongoing support and information helps women to 'hang in there', without this some women might not follow through all the processes it involves. (LADVC)

In terms of establishing the principle that domestic violence is a crime and should be taken more seriously by agencies, just under two-thirds thought DVM had some impact in this respect, but responses were more equivocal in relation to the impact on policing in particular. Here half of the groups thought DVM had, or had possibly, increased the willingness of police locally to arrest.

I have noticed that the police deal differently with women who have an advocate in DVM, but I've also noticed a more general change in attitude within the police, even their jargon has changed. (LBI Housing Officer)

Their presence makes a difference and they give women more confidence. (IVSS)

The final question probed what agencies thought about civilian crisis intervention teams being based in police stations. Several of the groups in this sample had been those raising concerns when DVM was being established. All of the respondents, apart from one who did not feel they could comment, strongly supported the concept.

I was unsure at first about them being in the police station, but it actually is very useful, it keeps the DVUs on their toes and gives clout with other agencies. (LBI Homelessness Officer)

For Black and ethnic minority communities, experiences with the police have not been good. Women basically do not trust the police, so having women there must be good. In Turkish culture it's not acceptable to involve the police (or any outsiders) in family matters, so dealing with non police women is better. (LBI Interpreting Service)

They are incredibly helpful and very supportive for women, especially those it is difficult to deal with, who for example have mental health problems. They are very patient and you can keep going back to them if you have to, they are open to listening and working as part of a team. (Hospital A&E Department)

DVM is a very useful and essential service, which has made my job much easier. (LBI Housing Officer)

It would be an absolute tragedy if they didn't continue; women in domestic violence relationships are notoriously difficult to reach without something like DVM to draw them into other services. (Women's Counselling Project)

DVM has helped other agencies focus on responses. Women have spoken very highly of them. We have got very used to them being here. If we suddenly got all the cases back it would be very difficult for us, particularly since they have raised awareness of the issue. DVM has made a great difference to women in this borough, providing out of hours practical support which no other agency does. (IVSS)

The 'clout' with other agencies was also noted by the DVM co-ordinator; rather than lessening DVM's credibility with other agencies being located in the police station enhanced it, enabling what she referred to as 'fast-tracking' access to support and resources.

Reflections on DVM's achievements in inter-agency work

The pressure of maintaining the service DVM offers, the limited movement in relation to law enforcement and the structural and inter-personal difficulties within DVM meant that the inter-agency co-ordination element of DVM's work was seldom prioritised or a core focus in management meetings, and the PMG was not successful in taking a lead role in this area. In the second interim evaluation report the possibility that the pilot had attempted to do too much in a limited time frame was noted; as was the way in which the structure of DVM management had not enabled strong formal developmental work with other agencies in the borough. Although there was, even at this point, evidence of strong links with some agencies and individuals, and the identification of, and response to, gaps in services.

Change, however, occurs in many and complex ways, and formal mechanisms are neither the only, nor even necessarily the most effective means. What the final round of agency interviews demonstrated was that through their crisis intervention work the DVM support workers had been quietly, but continuously, achieving the aim of increased co-ordination and consistent responses. Through their determination to ensure that women received quality of service, the most protection it was possible to create, and their statutory rights, DVM's workers influenced both the attitudes and responses of other agencies. It was their commitment, example and professional approach which made the difference, rather than the more obvious mechanisms of training and paper policies.

The effectiveness of the crisis intervention of DVM in creating change for individuals and within other agencies has implications for the development and extension of services in relation to domestic violence. The changes DVM created in other agencies came not from a project whose sole aim was to monitor and co-ordinate other agencies work (the model used in Duluth, Minnesota and Hamilton, New Zealand) but from working directly with women and acting as their advocate with all the other agencies which might enable them to move on. What the DVM pilot has demonstrated is another model of how to create local catalysts for change. This 'case advocacy' approach may have as much – and possibly in some cases more – influence than inter-agency fora. But these strategies should not be seen as either/or, the combination of a well resourced advocacy project with a resourced inter-agency forum would offer the most potential.

6 Telling the story – process evaluation

In writing this section I am acutely aware that it is impossible for an evaluator to know, let alone record, all of the processes involved in the establishment and life of even the most simple project. Not only is selection inevitable but also only a proportion of what happens is or becomes public knowledge. Process evaluations require interpretation, an exploration of the meaning and implications of events and interactions. This account is therefore limited by space, access, selection and interpretation. The emphasis is on the achievements of, and critical tensions within, the pilot project.

The focus is not individuals, since all the individuals involved adopted positions at times which hindered or enabled progress. Some individuals who were key in the early stages of the project subsequently left the borough. For those close to, and further away from any project the lessons learnt are those which transcend personalities and highlight more general themes and questions.

This chapter comprises several key elements: an account of the phases of the three year pilot; a description of how DVM operated in practice and concludes with reflections on some of the processes involved and lessons learnt. I have attempted to weave together multiple strands, each of which affects all the others: the work undertaken by DVM; relationships with the police and other agencies in the borough; how the staff team worked together; management of the project and external factors which had a critical bearing on DVM. The story is a complicated, and even at times, contradictory one.

Year one: setting up – starting out

The co-ordinator was appointed in October 1992, and the four support workers in January 1993. Following a month's induction DVM went 'live' in February 1993 and was in contact with 42 women in the first two weeks. The official launch of the project was high profile, and references to it in Hansard and by the Home Affairs Select Committee (1993) placed DVM in a local and national spotlight.

Developing crisis intervention

The most pressing immediate concerns were what appeared at the time as interminable delays in equipping the project – the car, direct telephone line, computers and communication equipment were not available until several months after service provision began. The first three months required considerable creativity and 'making do'. Since there was no similar project in Britain, and the available literature from Canada was decidedly short on details of what the crisis intervention actually comprised, there was a minimal knowledge/practice base to draw on. The DVM workers had to 'create' practice as they established the project. Initial enthusiasm and uncertainty about procedures resulted in several miscommunications between DVM and the police in the early weeks – on one occasion a support worker's request for assistance was understood as a major incident and a van load of police officers arrived! The later amusement caused by this story broke some ice between DVM and officers. All of these factors meant the co-ordinator worked extremely long hours during the first three months.

At an early stage the way DVM worked across the two divisions was re-negotiated. Co-ordinating split sites with a shift system that involved handover of work and a car proved impossible without considerable loss of hours, and duplication of all materials. The necessity in the first two months for overlapping shifts, in order that the workers could develop a sense of being part of a team, and innovative work practices, also supported a single base. DVM was, therefore, located in NI, for six months in a very small office, and in August 1993 the support workers moved into a large office with NIDVU. Referral routes for NH officers were developed. Whilst this created a viable office base for DVM, the loss of daily personal contact at NH was acknowledged (especially since the idea for the pilot had originated there).

At this initial stage administrative systems had to be developed which served a number of functions: organising the work of the project; recording it in such a way that it was possible for any worker to pick up on cases; tracking and monitoring work undertaken and the evaluation elements. DVM developed systems for: the allocation of shifts; logging work on shift; shift handovers; case notes; maintenance of the data base; and distribution of the evaluation questionnaire to service users.

After the initial period the support workers were on shift alone, and all had to be able to pick up on cases and work arising from a previous shift. Good practice protocols, amended and extended as the content of the work raised new issues, provided a basis for consistent responses, although each support worker developed their own personal 'style' within this. Weekly team meetings provided an essential meeting point for staff for both support and problem solving. Throughout the project the co-ordinator was available on bleep to discuss any immediate concerns or difficulties. Minor revisions to work practices were made after six months to ensure continuity (streamlining the daily log book, and having a short shift overlap). The work of DVM has been systematically recorded through these systems alongside the specially designed database. The policy and practice documents will be an invaluable resource for any other similar project. The administrative burden on the co-ordinator was recognised and funding for an administrator found towards the end of the first year (initially from the Islington Safer Cities Project, and for two years by PDU).

It soon became apparent that what may begin as a crisis response frequently involves lengthy follow-up work, in order to enable some kind of resolution. The extent of follow up support many women require led to a reassessment of the number of incidents it was reasonable for DVM to deal with effectively each week. Following several dangerous situations policy was amended to limit crisis call outs to the woman's home to cases where the perpetrator was arrested (previous policy only required that the perpetrator had left the home).

The need for cash for food and basic necessities for women who move into temporary accommodation outside office hours, especially over weekends, had not been anticipated. A 'victim's fund' was made possible by additional charitable funding. It was augmented by donations from several local businesses of baby equipment (nappies, milk etc.). This attention to the immediate, practical needs of service users is one of the strengths of DVM, since the minutiae of daily life make immediate change more or less of a possibility for individuals. Negotiating access to borough-wide schemes for alarms and telephone installation for 'vulnerable' people also reflect this attention to vital detail.

The staff team came from diverse backgrounds in a number of ways. The co-ordinator and one support worker had considerable professional experience in the area of domestic violence. All of the support workers underwent an appraisal after three months, and three were set targets for re-appraisal. By the end of the first year it had become clear that two of the staff team were unable to fulfil the diverse demands of the posts. In the first instance this was acknowledged by the individual herself, in the second a period of conflict ensued which was not possible to resolve amicably.

Relationships with the police

The idea for, and support of, DVM was primarily the preserve of senior police officers in the borough, and its funding was an achievement for them. Issues relating to the ownership of the project are discussed later in this section, here relationships with operational officers are discussed. In this initial period the primary issue was mutual suspicion, with both police officers and DVM staff having uncertainties in relation to each other.

Although an officer representing the DVUs (based at NI) had been a member of the steering group, and consultation on the proposal had taken place with them, much ground work had to be done to allay fears and misapprehensions. Ironically, given that DVM was based at NI, strong working relationships developed with the NHDVU very quickly, but the NI officers found it more difficult to explore how they might work effectively with DVM. Repeated staff changes made achieving this even more difficult. One obvious element was the extent of threat working with civilians and a high profile project represented. As important was the orientation of the two DVUs at the time. The two women officers at NH were anxious to increase law enforcement responses, including taking retrospective statements. They saw the support DVM offered as a resource which enabled them to concentrate on 'police' work. The NIDVU, in contrast, saw itself as offering 'victim support' and collating local domestic violence cases. Considerable time and effort was spent in the first months of the project to negotiate better and effective working relationships, but these had only marginally improved at NI when the support workers moved into a shared office with the DVU.

From the outset referral rates from police officers were variable, with some individuals being very committed to DVM and others not using it at all. Within a few months some officers had made strong enough links to drop into DVM's office to discuss cases. The co-ordinator noted that periods when referrals rose correlated with reminders through memos and briefings of DVM's presence and role. By the end of the year a drop in crisis referrals was being noted and raised in project meetings.

In planning DVM police training was considered an essential component, and a training needs analysis was mooted to be followed through by using regular training days. In the event the training was delayed and sessions limited to an hour which enabled little more than introducing DVM and the new divisional policy on domestic violence. Most of the operational officers in the two divisions had been briefed by the end of March. DVM's co-ordinator commented that reception ranged from "genuine interest to tired cynicism". Many were unfamiliar with the then force order and circular 60/1990 (a fact echoed by Grace [1995]). Developing a method for checking practice, particularly referral to DVM and reasons for non-arrest, was explored at an early stage. The fact that a common format could not be agreed between the divisions was one of the earliest examples of a recurrent theme. At NI all crime sheets were stamped (by DVM staff) with a block which listed the additional information needed, whilst at NH an existing proforma was amended. Inconsistencies rapidly emerged, and the resistance by most officers (and hostility amongst a section) to providing the required information meant the practice fell into disrepute after 12 months.

Regular review meetings between DVM, both DVUs and crime DCIs from both divisions were introduced as a mechanism for addressing 'teething problems'. At the first meeting doubts were expressed about: rationalising ways officers recorded domestic violence cases in both divisions; whether DVM had decreased the DVU work load; whether the time spent on individual cases was the most effective use of DVM; and whether DVM could/should work more collaboratively with both DVUs. Various proposals were discussed to increase co-operation, one of which was a combined Islington team comprising both DVUs and DVM.

Two other issues were significant for DVM in this period. A senior officer at NI who had taken responsibility for line management of the project, and had been a strong advocate and problem solver for it, left the borough. Subsequently line management was much more reactive, and consequently the advocate and problem solver position was less available to the project.

Both divisions were planning sectorisation at the time DVM was launched, but the process was more developed and implemented in NH in the first year (see Dixon, Kimber and Stanko (1993) for a discussion of the changes involved). This took precedence for the police for many months. In the surveys of police officers a significant proportion expressed concerns that one negative consequence of sectorisation might be increased response times. One definite consequence was that there were three local crime desk locations from which NHDVU officers had to collect crime sheets.

Relationships with other agencies

There was a mixed response to DVM from other agencies in the borough. Several – including Islington Victim Support Scheme (IVSS) – warmly welcomed the project and immediately established close working links. The majority took a 'wait and see' position; but there was a significant minority which expressed strong reservations. Two themes predominated – the location of the project in the police station which was seen as potentially compromising the autonomy of the workers and the allocation of major funding to something 'new' when funding for existing provision was inadequate and insecure. The local refuge and several other women's organisations were amongst the strongest sceptics.

The other local agencies with direct involvement in the criminal justice system – the CPS, the courts and probation were invited and encouraged to take part in developing a local culture of change. Responses were varied, with probation being the only agency which felt able/was willing to commit itself to a partnership with DVM. Even here, however, an internal agenda – the desire to develop work with domestic violence offenders – predominated in this early period.

Positive collaborative work with the LADVC emerged rapidly in the form of a joint questionnaire which combined her needs with that of the evaluation. This was followed by a joint enterprise with DVM; producing a local information and advice booklet for women suffering domestic violence. The process of developing referral routes for DVM's users involved both discovering what was available and making personal contact with service providers. Daily practice was combined with the results from the evaluation survey of agencies to produce the first version of DVM's referral directory.

Project management

It was at the level of project management that the most intractable difficulties were experienced in the first few months of DVM's existence. Movement from a steering group to the intended management structure had begun before the pilot started and a Management Committee – without its full complement of members, and retaining many of the original police membership (albeit that some had the status of observers) – was instituted in the summer of 1992. As members from outside the police joined, questions about the number of police members were raised, within a broader discussion about extending partnership beyond the initial proposers, if the intention of inter-agency management and the aim of enhancing responses of other agencies were to be achieved. This became an area of intense conflict and contest, which despite numerous formal and informal attempts could not be resolved. The issue dominated management meetings for several months and resulted in an atmosphere of anxiety, mistrust and on occasion open hostility.

The failure of the Management Committee to resolve the issue resulted in a proposal from PDU for a revised structure in early 1993. The two police divisions and the co-sponsorship of the Islington Safer Cities Project had made issues of accountability complex. This new structure involved an Executive Group (EG) whose members would be a police representative, Safer Cities (as the two proposers), probation, a local authority representative, DVM's treasurer and the project consultant. The EG was chaired by PDU, its function defined as ensuring that DVM was keeping to set aims, objectives, timetables and budget. The EG had one sub-group – Employment and Finance – which had responsibility for recruitment, other employment issues and monitoring income and expenditure.

A Programme Management Group (PMG) replaced the advisory group, which had not at this point been formally established. The PMG drew membership from the statutory and voluntary sectors, but unlike the previous advisory group it had decision-making powers, and a full and sub-group structure. The PMG's remit specified that it had responsibility to the EG, and was charged with a number of responsibilities including: implementing and developing the aims of the project and the priorities and tasks agreed by the EG; advising the EG where decisions may involve a shift from the original aims; identifying needs for additional resources and fund-raising; identifying and monitoring work of the sub-groups. The original intention was that much of the developmental work would take place in sub-groups of which four were specified initially: equal opportunities; legal response; operations and practice; and charities. The latter was to have a limited life in order to obtain charitable status.

The co-ordinator, evaluator and project consultant attended both groups. Whilst there was some initial resistance to this restructuring, it did shift the project out of a difficult impasse and meant that more detailed policy and practice matters were subsequently addressed. Some of the dynamics and processes involved are explored further in the reflections section at the end of this chapter.

The PMG was established in May 1993 with a broad and expanding membership. Initial meetings involved informing members about the project, the remit of the PMG and developing membership and participation. Most members expressed support for DVM, and a wish to be part of developing responses in the borough. Within four months three task orientated groups were established: Operations and Practice; Policy; and Legal Response.

The servicing of both groups, and the sub-groups was the responsibility of the project co-ordinator, and the appointment of an administrator was in part recognition of the work involved.

The management of the project in its first months added to, rather than resolved, the teething problems inevitable in new projects. The pre-occupation with ownership and position meant that many of the pressing policy and practical matters either took a back seat or simply 'fell off' the agenda. For example, drafting the policy guidelines on how the police and DVM were to work together, a task set for completion before the appointment of support workers, took over five months to complete.

Summary

The first year of DVM was a complex mixture of achievement, effort and determination on the one hand and tension, lost opportunities and unnecessary delays and confusions on the other. New projects are inevitably beset by practical problems; translating an idea from paper into a reality reveals needs and complications which could not have been anticipated.

Year two: digging in

The second year was a period of consolidation and change. Consolidation of the principles and practice of crisis intervention and working links with the police and other agencies in the borough; change in terms of project staff, of personnel at many levels within the police – at both DVUs, the Chief Superintendent at NI – and establishing a daily presence at NH. The issues of power, position and control were not an overt feature, but recurred in less obvious ways.

Direct service provision

At the start of the second year a new member of the team – the administrator – joined, and two support workers had left and been replaced. A third vacancy occurred when the newest appointee was offered another job. This period of staff change was unsettling for the project, but it is to the credit of the co-ordinator and support workers that the impact on both the service and the project as a whole was kept to a minimum, and a strong sense of being a team re-emerged. The evaluations of women users (see Chapter Three) continued to be extremely positive.

As of 17 August 1994 the DVM database contained records of 807 cases (individuals in contact with the project) and 919 incidents which had been responded to. The average of new cases per month was 42, and of incidents 50. This is a minimal figure, however, since limited contact cases are not entered. Despite this caveat the number of cases was half the target set in the early months. The majority of DVM's police referrals were from NI, and this became increasingly the case.

The major concern throughout the year was a drop in crisis referrals (and limited use of DVM by NH officers) and the implications of this for DVM, given that it represents one of the unique elements of the project. The issue was raised by the co-ordinator at EG and DVM/DVU review meetings throughout the year. Various reasons were proffered by police officers to explain the decrease, from the limited memory of police officers, the turn over of new staff each year, through to the fact that DVM had decreased confidence in the service or alternatively had been so successful within a year that need had decreased substantially!

The process of moving from recognition of the problem within the police through to action being taken was more protracted than necessary, but a number of strategies were adopted throughout 1994. These included: a session with supervisory officers at NI; re-briefings of beat officers in both divisions at training/sector days; a notice on DVM's service; making contact with the control room (where calls to the police are processed) when DVM shifts began, and ensuring that the referral protocol was understood.

Whilst each of these had an immediate effect, none were sustained over time, and the drop from NH was particularly noticeable. An effort to increase crisis referrals from NH had an effect in May/June, during which time a meeting took place between DVM's co-ordinator and NH's Chief Superintendent. Sustaining the changes was explored in terms of visibility and regular contact at NH, and at this meeting a decision was made to move the support workers' evening shift (6pm to 2am) to NH.

Both the workers and the evaluator expressed reservations initially. The concerns of the workers centred on the absence of an office, the delay in installing a dedicated phone line, and the lack of privacy. Whilst these were significant, especially early on in the change, there were undoubted gains in the personal contact with officers at NH. The evaluator raised the danger of losing more referrals from NI than would be gained from NH, and the loss of contact with current 'clients' who often phoned in the evening for advice, reassurance and moral support. This latter point was recognised as a significant loss in an assessment of the change by the workers. One commented later:

> We have done lot of good work through our presence at NH, you have to be there, be part of the team for them to own you. But we have lost contact with women, and in terms of working practice it's not ideal that they ring and get a message saying phone another number – when you are distressed you don't get a pen in case there is an answerphone message, do you? (SW3)

In formal interviews the support workers were unanimous that their work was challenging and that establishing something new, with no model of how to do it, had created opportunities to develop new skills and different ways of working. The difficulties they had encountered centred on finding ways to work within an institution which they worked in but did not fully belong to. The ambivalence to their presence amongst some police officers, and occasional outright hostility was the most problematic element of their work.

By this stage the DVM support workers had developed a model of crisis intervention in relation to domestic violence, which is different from other services to date in Britain, and what they have learnt and recorded in the revised good practice guidelines represents a potentially lasting contribution to the field. Although the number of cases dealt with each month is significantly lower than the optimum possible, it is nonetheless substantially greater than the numbers most refuges can offer substantial support to over the same time period. The local VSS also publicly acknowledged in a PMG meeting that they could neither respond to this number of cases, nor offer the same quality of service. These facts alone illustrate that DVM was providing an additional, and different option, and highlights the need for this type of option within a comprehensive service to women experiencing domestic violence.

Relationships with the police

As DVM became securer in its structure, practice and location, strong positive working relationships with both individual officers and sections of the police developed.

During the second year staff changes at both DVUs resulted in an interesting reversal of the picture from the first year. At NI the placing of investigative officers within the DVU shifted emphasis to law enforcement and the fact that DVM could pick up on advice and support was welcomed by most of the officers in the Unit. The sharing of an office also facilitated this changing relationship and several of the officers in formal interviews paid tribute to the DVM staff, and what they had learnt from them. For example:

> *When I first went to the DVU I went with an open mind – or I tried to have an open mind. But I must admit that after being there a month or so my whole attitude totally changed. I was able to spend a lot more time with the victims, appreciate their point of view more, especially with the help of the DVM girls. I thought this is a really brilliant project, and I got so I really enjoyed dealing with domestic violence! I used to be one of those officers who when I got in in the morning and saw news of a domestic, prisoner in the bin, I used to think 'here we go, you do all the work and then a week later she'll say she wants to drop it'.*

> *The best thing was I was able to do my job, be sympathetic, but remain impartial as an investigator, because DVM were there to take them under their wing give them more sympathy and all the support that they required. In that respect DVM took a hell of a lot of pressure off me as the investigating officer. Things like accommodation, if we could get the victim away from where the perpetrator can get at her, we found*

once we could do that many more women were willing to go to court, substantiate the allegation, which for me was great. I just hope to God the government decides to fund it for a lot longer, because the benefits certainly that the victims I've dealt with have had, have certainly been great.

In contrast the new staff at NH had shifted from a law enforcement model to one which stressed victim support, and unlike their predecessors, clearly found working alongside DVM difficult. This reversal of orientations within the DVUs coupled with changed relationships with DVM suggests that where DVUs are based on a victim support model projects like DVM are likely to be perceived as threatening, as 'taking away' work from the specialist police officers. In contrast where the DVU emphasises law enforcement the availability of trained civilians who undertake the victim support aspects of work is both welcomed and valued.[33]

The review meetings in this period, with a problem-solving co-operative framework, were more positive but less frequent. DVU officers commented that they were more able to pursue investigations, and that arrests had increased and withdrawals decreased. Open and honest minuted discussions occurred about NH DVU's fears of having their work and role taken over (they did in fact offer support establishing DVM's night shift at the station). On another occasion following the lack of use of a log recording the daily work of both DVUs (designed by the evaluator after agreement from and consultation with both DVUs) concerns about being themselves under scrutiny were acknowledged.

A number of factors – the basic service being established, the availability of back and current data, responses in police questionnaires for the evaluation, repeat briefings to officers – contributed evidence of variability in police practice. Some of the shortcomings noted related to elements of force policy, as well as limited movement on divisional policy in relation to the law enforcement element of DVM's aims (see Chapter Four).

That DVM (either through the staff team or the evaluation) continued to raise the issue of inconsistency in police responses frequently resulted in irritation, and on occasion hostility, from the police side which made joint action towards resolution difficult. The persistence which was necessary to keep the law enforcement response on the agenda was wearing and not always followed through by the police or DVM management. For example, the need for additional police training was highlighted in DVM co-ordinators' quarterly reports and the first interim evaluation report. An hour was allocated by one division, and little if anything done in the other. This limited response was not addressed formally by the EG.

---

33 These two approaches – law enforcement and victim support – were highlighted in an internal police review of DVU's conducted by Sgt Shirley Tulloch in 1993/4, but this study has not been published.

On occasion co-operative explorations through debate and discussion took place in which two angles on the same problem were recognised. But more commonly interactions were conflictual, constructed as opposing sides. A pattern emerged whereby DVM would table issues of concern; in the discussion which followed (this could occur within an individual meeting or over time) the validity of the concerns would be questioned, and 'hard' evidence requested (even when what was at issue was precisely the lack of accurate data to assess police practice). Once some validity was granted explanations would be offered which deflected attention from police practice. When an issue was acknowledged movement towards action often occurred with minimal exploration of the costs and benefits of this change to the police themselves, to DVM and to service users. Police culture is one which prioritises action, in which it is presumed that if there is a rule/policy officers follow it unless proven otherwise. At the same time there is strong resistance to accepting any such 'proof' and a defensiveness when shortcomings are revealed. Whilst this response to scrutiny of practice is not confined to the police – in most large agencies such 'exposure' results in defensive responses – there is a particularity in how the police react. When a concern was accepted the outcome tended to be the creation of an immediate change to 'put it right', get rid of the problem, rather than explore what created it in the first place.

A graphic example of this was the 'crime sheet issue'. There was evidence of differential implementation of completing crime sheets for all domestic incidents in the pre-DVM police data (see Table 4.1), and DVM's briefing of officers and the evaluation questionnaires revealed several problems; resistance by officers to, and resentment of, the practice where the incident is not (according to them) a crime. If officers chose to use other methods of recording there was a potential loss of cases following police management decisions (since cases were supposed to be on crime sheets) to no longer require DVU officers to trawl CAD records. This issue had implications for accurate data, referrals to DVM, follow up by DVUs and monitoring of local practice.

Initial responses were to deny that it was a problem, despite some officers publicly and privately admitting that they did not always complete crime sheets. When the problem was acknowledged at a formal meeting one senior officer later decided to issue a memo discontinuing completion of crime sheets in his division for domestic disputes which would be recorded on CAD only with details sent daily to the DVU. This hastily made decision went against force policy, and created further differences between the two divisions. The decision was reversed but in the process further confusion and no doubt resentment was created amongst beat officers.

What was never adequately explored were the underlying issues, the reasons for officers' resistance. That this continued to remain a burning issue amongst police officers was confirmed when it was passionately raised in 1995 briefing sessions and both the evaluation focus groups done in 1995. The possibility of developing/using forms designed specifically to address domestic violence cases was never been fully discussed, despite examples being made available through the evaluation.[34]

During this year the DVU at NI had their remit extended to encompass racial attacks.

Inter-agency links

DVM's second year marked the emergence of increased confidence in referrals to and advocacy with other agencies, and the establishment of strong connections and alliances with some, including a number of the initial sceptics.

The increasing awareness amongst the support workers of which agencies worked best with domestic violence meant referrals were more selective, and where needed (for example, by disabled and/or ethnic minority women) more specialised. The database shows 90 different agencies were referred to over the whole pilot, with increasing variation in the second and third years, including local groups offering longer term counselling support.

Advocacy skills also developed, and the frequent contact with some agencies – such as housing officers – undoubtedly resulted in better practice. From DVM's perspectives knowing not only procedures for temporary accommodation and housing transfers, but also named individuals, meant that the process could be speeded up for some women.

Ongoing connections were maintained, and even enhanced in some cases and new links established. Particularly significant here was the hospital accident and emergency department, which by the end of the second year was contacting DVM to visit women who arrived for treatment for injuries; itself a form of crisis for the victim. Most notably by the end of the second year the local refuge was regularly attending and contributing to PMG meetings having re-assessed their doubts about the police station location, and had become a supporter of DVM's contribution to services in the borough.

---

34   Just after the end of the PDU funded pilot both divisions were computerised using a system called CRIS. Only crimes are recorded on this system; it is an open question whether and how domestic violence calls which are not defined as crimes will be recorded.

All of these developments were either the outcome of the contacts made during crisis intervention referrals and advocacy, or the energy DVM put into establishing and maintaining contact with other agencies.

Management and structure

The line management of DVM moved to the head of the police area child protection team. It became clear during the year that the officer saw her role in a much more limited way than her predecessor had. Her relative separation from routine operational issues also limited her ability to act as an advocate for the project amongst frontline officers and their managers. The absence of effective line management was not addressed by the EG until the final year. One of the support workers reflecting on this period said:

> *The management could have been better, there has been lots of confusion about line management. Our original line manager was very approachable, we lost a lot when he left. We were under the impression that that role was being taken over, but that wasn't the other person's understanding. That made the team more isolated in the station and that could have been eased.* (SW4)

The overall management of DVM continued to be a two tier structure,with PDU chairing the EG; although by the end of the year a plan for the chair to be taken by the two original proposers of the project – the police and the Islington Safer Cities Project (by the point this happened the project had become Safer Islington) had been accepted.

The relative absence of conflictual rivalry in the EG meetings was the outcome of both the assumption of the chair by PDU and the responsibility which an ongoing project creates and demands. The EG had a core of consistent members, although the minimal participation of a local authority representative was striking. There was more than one occasion where the non-attendance of a key member prevented issues being resolved, and with quarterly meetings this resulted in long delays.

Recruitment to the PMG continued throughout the second year, priority being to recruit more members from ethnic minority groups. Serious attempts were made to create an effective body, with substitution being discouraged. There was a notional membership of 20, but despite the best intentions of DVM attendance was variable and seldom consistent; different agencies would attend and some agencies regularly sent different individuals (including the police and the CPS). This inconsistency meant that a proportion of most meetings involved 'treading water' – going over basic issues and previous discussions. As a consequence the PMG was never in a position to take the kinds of responsibility envisaged for it. The sub-group structure also reflected this variable commitment. The policy group did complete the task of producing a policy document on confidentiality, but undertook no other work of substance. The legal sub-group had both a brief and issues of substance to work on raised by both the evaluation and DVM's daily work. Little was achievable, however, since the same members from the police and CPS never attended more then one meeting, and frequently sent apologies. After two successive meetings at which the only attenders were DVM's co-ordinator, the evaluator and the project consultant (and considerable efforts being made in between the two meetings to ensure better attendance at the second) the group was more or less disbanded.

There are several factors which may have contributed to this element of the project structure not working. At the point at which the PMG was established the legacies of disputed power and control still remained in the EG, and at times split over into PMG meetings, to the extent that management issues rather than strategic and policy development took precedence. At this point the PMG became caught up in disputing the same areas of power as the EG, rather than finding its own base of power within the overall project. The involvement and commitment of the statutory sector, especially the other criminal justice system agencies and the local authority, was limited, in contrast to the far less resourced voluntary sector groups. Questions about whether members were recruited from the right level in their agencies, and whether the PMG was perceived as not having decision-making powers, and therefore an 'unimportant' body, are also relevant here. It is undoubtedly the case that the early difficulties the project experienced in terms of structure and management had an impact long after they were formally resolved. In retrospect it could be argued that more emphasis should have been given to involving all the criminal justice agencies in the structure of DVM more effectively, since they were crucial to one of the core aims of the project. However, this may have required a trade off in relation to the crisis intervention element, which required building co-operative relationships with a much broader range of local agencies.

The second interim evaluation report noted the limits of the two tier structure and the absence of an appropriate route for the follow through of detailed matters of policy and practice, resulting in an immense responsibility for the co-ordinator, who during this period, was also not having regular line management. Her invidious position required strong and effective management input. Many of the concerns raised about limited movement on some of the aims of the project involved current police practice. Pushing on these by DVM staff was in tension with the necessity of developing and maintaining cordial day to day relationships with police officers. DVM was a small non-hierarchical project located within a large hierarchical organisation, not noted for its ability to accommodate change easily or rapidly, especially when the impetus is perceived to come from the 'outside'. There was a pressing need for an effective formal mechanism through which policy and practice issues could be examined and addressed, through which DVM staff could be seen as acting from a mandate with explicit, ongoing high level police support. Such a group was proposed in the second interim evaluation report, but was never created.

Commentary

The form and level of commitment to DVM varied between the two police divisions and over time, and at least 12 senior officers had some level of involvement in, and responsibility for, the project during the first two years. Whilst this breadth of ownership was welcomed, on more than one occasion the input involved minimal understanding of the aims and origins of the project and was more about 'making a mark' – asserting some kind of authority over how DVM developed in ways which would have either compromised its relative autonomy (a model in which DVM co-worked all cases alongside police officers in a unified borough wide unit) or re-invented it in altered form (only providing immediate crisis intervention). On at least two occasions DVM was caught between competing and incompatible views of future developments in the borough (the crime sheet issue and proposals for the unified Domestic Violence Unit).

Mark Liddle and Lorraine Gelsthorpe (1994) also reflect on this area. In their experience whilst the police were always "key players" in inter-agency work, there were frequently different levels of commitment across divisions and uneven ownership within them.

Large agencies such as the police are usually characterised by internal divisions across departments, and by competition among these for status and resources; these factors may lead to an unevenness of commitment and ownership within each agency. (p27)

They make the telling point that whilst high level resolution of issues are not necessarily easily implemented, sustained high level support within agencies for new ways of working are a necessary component of any partnership aimed at change.

Whilst police use of DVM was addressed throughout the period a similar amount of time and energy was not devoted to issues of inconsistent police practice, or the lack of regular statistics to monitor law enforcement. Moreover, in addressing the decline in crisis referrals attention focused on how DVM could/should encourage officers, including making substantial changes to DVM's ways of working (such as the move to NH). Despite these many attempts to adapt to police modes of operation, and spending time developing more personal contacts with individual officers, a perception persisted amongst some officers of DVM as somehow 'anti-police'. The culture of police stations – within which rumour and gossip thrive – is not an easy one in which to establish new ways of working. More emphasis from the police side on the feedback to officers from the victims on what they valued in both police and DVM responses, on how DVM created more faith in the police, would have been an asset at this stage.[35]

The other issue which DVM was unable to resolve effectively was how to create effective management structures whilst recruiting a broad membership to the project as a whole. The experience of DVM was that these proved to be incompatible goals. However, the issues of how to create effective management structures and the variable commitment and input from Management Committee and advisory group members is not confined to DVM, but a critical tension which affects thousands of independent and voluntary sector projects.

Year three: difficult endings, new beginnings

The final year of the pilot was marked by a further series of changes in police personnel and practices, a decline not just in referrals to the project, but also of domestic violence calls to the police (especially in NI), stronger working relationships with the police, and a crisis of sorts within the staff team.

Service provision

Having developed an effective new form of service provision, the last year was one of frustration for the DVM team. They knew that the content and quality of what they offered was valued by women, but the decline in referrals meant they were often under used. One support worker commented:

> *Where they arrest they don't always get in touch with us, and that is very frustrating, because that is our role. Too often they [police officers] treat it as a one off thing and want to get out as quickly as possible, not using all the options they have.* (SW3)

This was especially the case for night shifts at NH. Whilst for the first six months of the experiment contact with the officers was useful in building relationships, and in providing time to discuss police response, on too many

---

35 All of the evaluation questionnaires promised feedback to officers, and both interim reports suggested ways this might best be done. Despite meetings between the evaluator and police officers who would create the written material, to my knowledge no feedback (apart from the two focus groups in 1995) has been given

evenings it was 'dead' time; waiting for calls with no access to the project office where other tasks could be completed. The NH shift was discontinued towards the end of the pilot.

The under use of the project was dispiriting for the workers, and the looming end of the pilot added to a sense of discontent – at having established something unique, whilst having an uncertain, and possibly no, future. Disagreement emerged within the team about whether DVM should continue to keep to its original brief, or find other referral routes and do developmental work in the community for the remaining months.

These factors combined with a perception, amongst the support workers, of being excluded from the decision-making processes of the project (the co-ordinator was intended to be the conduit between the staff team and the EG and vice versa) and that their work was not valued. Much of the last six months were marked by tension and at times dissension in the staff team. Asked if under-use was an underlying issue, one support worker said:

> *There is an awful lot of time on our hands to think about things. If we were really really busy there would be less frustration and less time to think. But maybe it is good to think about them... I think if there were a clearer flow of information and more of a dialogue, people just need to be heard. And even if they are being heard, but feel they are not, then those perceptions need to change.* (SW1)

Attempts initially by the co-ordinator and then by management to resolve the dissension were unsuccessful, although key decisions were made. In a meeting with the evaluator requested by the support workers, it became clear that some of the distress hinged on a sense that any 'failure' attributed to the project would be located in the staff team, and that their ideas about how adaptions could be made in the final year had not been taken seriously. This conflict did not, however, appear to affect service provision to women. During the last year the DVM workers also had to cope with three deaths of women they had worked with: two were murdered and one committed suicide.

Relationships with the police

Throughout the pilot project decisions were made by the police which had direct consequences for DVM, with minimal if any consultation. The decision to include racial assaults in the brief of NIDVU was one example, closely followed by an announcement that in January 1995 NIDVU would become a 'Vulnerable Persons Unit' (VPU). The potential implications for DVM were extensive, but neither the staff team nor the EG were invited to discuss the proposal before the decision was made.

The increased staffing of the VPU (from 4 to 9 officers) and the change in working hours (up to 10pm and including weekend shifts) both reflected awareness of the effectiveness of DVM and, in the event, resulted in even stronger co-ordination between police officers and the project. Three of the support workers reflected on this changed context:

> *They hear us working every day, how we talk with women, ask them what they want, stressing it's not their fault – all the things we say to women in a crisis. So they hear that difference, day in day out, it's water washing over stone.* (SW1)

> *The longer we've been here we've sort of been absorbed in the paintwork for some officers. We don't stand out so much any more as different, so we have won our spurs in that sense.* (SW4)

> *It feels like a lot has changed just recently, especially with the police. At the beginning there were lots of changes when we were setting up the project, and a hostile and suspicious response. I remember that sense of hostility in the first year very strongly, but we were very busy. Then we went through a quiet period, staff changes. For me the most positive changes have been in the last six months. We have integrated more and been accepted more. With the VPU we liaise constantly, often work together on cases, consult each other – we are not doing each other's work, but organising our respective work better.* (SW3)

These were substantial achievements, but the ironies of better working relationships at the same time as not being consulted about major changes in policy and lower referrals were not lost on the DVM team.

The other significant factor during this period was wider changes influencing police responses to domestic violence. Two agreements between the police and the CPS had (and have) potentially huge implications. The 'charging standards' agreement involved agreeing common definitions for a variety of criminal offences. They were introduced to provide common guidance to police and prosecutors on the most appropriate charge, in the hope that this would decrease the perceived need in the CPS to alter charges laid. One element involved a re-definition of 'common assault', which importantly is not an arrestable offence. Many of the visible injuries – at the point police arrive – which victims of domestic violence sustain will undoubtedly fall into this category; raising complex issues about policies which encourage arrest. The 'case disposal' system was introduced in 1995. It requires that officers go through a routine process before converting an arrest into a charge. This process involves assessing the relative significance of various 'aggravating' and 'mitigating' factors, with the balance determining whether a charge will be laid. Numbers are assigned to these factors, counting them up, subtracting aggravating from mitigating, resulting in a figure which determines whether a charge will be laid; 5 or 4 is always a charge, 3 is marginal, and 2 and 1 mean no charge will be laid, although cautions may be issued in some circumstances.

Whilst there are strong arguments for police officers routinely assessing their decision-making,[36] there are potential implications for domestic violence in the aggravating and mitigating factors. Whilst several of the aggravating factors can be applied to domestic violence, so too can most of the mitigating ones. In fact a number of the latter provide officers with exactly the same reasons they have traditionally used not to proceed with cases. For example: the offence is "trivial" and likely to attract a small or nominal penalty; the offence was committed whilst under provocation, was an impulsive response; the offender shows genuine remorse, apologises to the victim and offers to participate in rehabilitation/referral schemes or seek medical help. This last factor is particularly alarming, since it constitutes informal diversion, with minimal if any mechanisms for ensuring that the promise has been kept. The Chief Superintendent in one of the divisions recognised the potential contradiction between case disposal and local policy on domestic violence and reached an agreement with the local CPS that domestic violence could be defined, for his division, as a "locally prevalent offence" – an aggravating factor. However, only a minority of the case disposal forms in the CPS files from that division had this marked as an aggravating factor (see Chapter Four).

The implications of charging standards and case disposal, singly and in combination, for treating domestic violence as a serious crime[37] are extensive, but have not been a matter of public debate.

Throughout the pilot no mechanism was ever developed for effective tracking of police practice. Both DVUs were resistant to additional work, and it was never the remit of either DVM or the evaluator to track all cases from two divisions. Whilst both DVUs maintained that they could produce figures, these were not routinely made available to the EG, and were only compiled in early 1995 by one division following a recommendation in the second interim evaluation report (see Chapter Four).

Management and structure

The two tier management structure was unwieldy, and the PMG never fulfilled the hopes and intentions invested in it. Following a recommendation in the second interim evaluation report, for the last six months of the pilot the EG

---

36 A number of officers did, however, comment on the additional paper work that case disposal involves, since it is a seperate form and has to be completed.

37 The principle that domestic violence is a crime has been endorsed by both the Home Office and Scottish Office, and formed the basic message of short public education campaigns in 1994/5

and PMG combined into a single Management Committee, chaired jointly by the two proposers. Attendance at meetings was better, and some former PMG members became stalwart participants. The pressure of the tensions within the staff team and the impending demise of the project if further funding could not be found, resulted in more frequent meetings, and occasionally fraught and bad-tempered interactions. However, this group was successful in obtaining some continuation funds, and it continues to manage the project.

Reflections - the 'p' word

From the outset the key internal issue which provoked both debate and at times disagreement has been 'ownership': within and between the police; between the police and other agencies; and within the staff team. These differences hinge fundamentally on power, but were seldom openly acknowledged as such. Indeed the concepts of 'ownership', 'partnership' and 'inter-agency working' provide a language in which power is an implicit rather than explicit theme. At a meeting organised to resolve the early internal difficulties one senior police officer admitted that power and "competing for it" had been the underlying problem.

The ways in which power was used, contested and challenged in the process of establishing and maintaining this project are multiple and complex, and cannot be reduced to the behaviour of individuals. Many individuals shifted their positions and behaviour over time. The processes were intricate and at times perplexing, since what appeared at one point to be a resolution/compromise were subsequently disputed. Rather than provide a narrative account, four forms of power which played a part in these dynamics are highlighted: institutional; formal; gender; and interpersonal. They are explored using the concept of locating oneself in a position in relation to power, with examples from the various phases of DVM. This analysis is intended to provide access to the unspoken dynamics which underpinned the tensions, and is offered as a framework for conceptualising these issues which may be useful tools in other contexts.

Institutional power

DVM was located within an extremely powerful, hierarchical and traditionally male-dominated institution. The police service has, moreover, during the last decade, been the subject of considerable critical attention, and domestic violence has been one area where substantial criticism of police response has been made, and claims made more recently about significant change.

The centrality of the police to the project is not simply that DVM was located in the police, but that the police were also its original proposers. The partnership they entered into when applying for PDU funding was with a small agency – the Islington Safer Cities Project – which had, of necessity built strong working relationships with the police and had a limited life span. The police were not just joint proposers, but in effect the 'senior partner', having both more to gain and more to lose. Furthermore, the funding of DVM by PDU was clearly considered significant by senior police officers outside the borough, which in various ways and at different times influenced events. The establishment, and hopefully success, of DVM 'mattered' intensely to all key participants, but perhaps especially to the police.

This was, in fact, acknowledged both within the steering group and the nascent Management Committee, and discussions took place repeatedly about how this could be recognised, whilst at the same time safeguarding the relative autonomy of DVM and the necessity of moving towards some form of wider 'partnership' and 'community ownership' as outlined in the project proposal. The point at which consensus broke down was in this transition process, and the position of chair was the 'issue' on which different perspectives on ownership and power emerged. The insistence of the police that they should retain the chair was both justified and contested in institutional terms.

The impasse this created was only resolved by use of the countervailing institutional power of PDU. Whilst this undoubtedly resolved the deadlock (and it may have been the only way forward at the time), it simultaneously reinforced the centrality of institutional power and particular forms of 'ownership'.

The selection of membership for the MC and then EG was made on the basis of individual's having institutional power, in the hope of creating a linked dynamic of change. Not all members carried this commitment through and DVM was not able to create formal mechanisms to ensure this occurred. The new EG structure also resulted in the loss of key representatives from the CPS and health authority; the former since the observer status they had opted for was incompatible with the function of the new group, the latter because the health authority was not considered central to the project aims.

There are complex questions raised by this process for the structure, practices and evaluation of inter-agency initiatives:

• Are there fundamental differences between inter-agency projects which originate from powerful, statutory institutions and ones which begin in the community/voluntary sector in terms of whether, and how widely, 'partnerships' and power-sharing can develop?

- Are there structural components in the establishment of projects which reinforce existing power relations or facilitate more co-operative working? For example, can a project which was initially 'owned' by two agencies become 'owned' by many more, if all or some of the originators do not demonstrate a wish to share (if not give up) the position of 'senior partner'?

- What conditions enable individuals who both have, and are used to using, institutional power, to use it for the good of project, and if necessary take back challenges to their own organisations?

- Does establishing decision-making by consensus inadvertently serve to cement the power of particular members who are willing and able to use institutional power to block decisions which would otherwise be agreed?

- Should individuals be invited to participate solely on the basis of their position within institutional hierarchies, or should more attempt be made to discover who the 'change makers' are within institutions?

What difference would an explicit recognition of power and hierarchies, and a commitment to working with the difficulties and contradictions inherent in them, make to inter-agency work?

Formal power

This concept refers to the positions individuals have within particular institutions, and within the structure of DVM.

In common with many other hierarchical organisations, deference to one's superiors is expected in the police. Where opinions/positions were articulated by a senior officer, their juniors, despite having a somewhat different perspective were seldom free to voice this publicly. Differences between the police participants were thus minimised, creating an illusion of a united position.[38]

At all stages of the pilot individual police officers of various ranks and orientations to DVM were connected to it. Some voiced strong commitment to building partnerships with other agencies and the wider community and saw DVM as one way to explore new forms of policing, others were more concerned to be attached to a project with institutional and wider public significance.

---

38   This was reflected in the two focus groups conducted for the evaluation; supervisors took most of the speaking time, and beat officers tended to contribute when they were able to agree with or expand on what had previously been said.

The early crisis was precipitated when successive attempts at mediation and possible compromise were undermined by an individual senior police officer at subsequent meetings. At two points where resolution was possible, albeit through formal means, rather than consensus, the process was interrupted by a resort to 'formal constitutionalism' by the then police chair. This series of difficult, and at points unpleasant, meetings created a conflict situation where power was contested but seldom discussed explicitly.

Formal power was also involved in internal discussions and debates within and between the local police divisions as to where DVM should be located. Proposals were made by middle managers to locate DVM in the child protection/community liaison section, and within a proposed division wide unified domestic violence team. Both were rejected by more senior officers. Subsequent decisions about changing the remit of NIDVU also involved the formal power invested in senior police officers to make operational decisions without reference to DVM.

There were many other examples of formal power affecting the development of DVM. Two further examples were: the issues raised by the support workers towards the end of the pilot involving what they perceived as their exclusion from formal power; the possibility of the LADVC joining the EG being rejected on the grounds that her formal power was limited (the member who had formal power seldom attended meetings, and the LADVC was a local change maker in relation to domestic violence).

The early difficulties of DVM in relation to both institutional and formal power created a context in which a desire to minimise conflict predominated in subsequent management meetings.

Gender power

Threading through the establishment of DVM are complex gender issues; in relation to the issue of domestic violence, how it might be best responded to, and in terms of the interactions between key individuals connected to the project, and within their own agencies. The decision to build a Management Committee of strategically placed individuals from other agencies, who have the possibility of creating change in them, inevitably meant that they were more likely to be men; although attempts were made to request, where possible, female representatives. The reconstituted EG did in fact have a majority of female members.

At the initial stage (and to a lesser extent subsequently) some of the problematic dynamics within the management of the project linked to gender in two ways. Firstly, much of the tone and style in which disagreements were played out took the form of established masculine norms of power broking, where conflicts are frequently resolved outside formal meetings, over drinks or in other locations women are less likely to frequent. Secondly, this 'business as usual' model was contested by several strong women who took a position of principle that disagreements and difficulties should be honestly and openly debated. This does not mean that whenever there was an issue of dispute the sides were drawn between men and women (this was seldom, if ever, the case), but that there were significant differences about *how* organisations operate, *how* power is allocated and used. Where these differences emerge explicitly, and they are increasingly doing so within and between organisations, they confound the local informal practices and networks (usually male) which have developed to resolve tensions. This raises complex issues about how 'partnerships' are constructed, in which interpersonal and inter-agency dynamics and rivalries are but one component.

There were also differences in understandings of the relevance of gender to the issue of domestic violence. Some members of the steering group put forward the view that it would be "sexist" if the DVM workers were all women, and indeed that there 'ought' to be at least one male member of the team. This position both ignored the fact that the vast majority of victims of domestic violence are female and that they, in the main, express a strong preference for being supported by women and suggested that criteria other than experience and skills should be used in recruitment.

At the management level the opposite point was made very strongly, and had majority support, in the early days; that it was symbolically important for DVM to have a non-police and female chair. The fact that the PDU staff were both female temporarily resolved the issue. When the chair reverted to the MC, for strategic reasons it was agreed that the two original proposers should share it. Whilst there was no opposition to this expressed, nonetheless the consequence was that gender power merged with, rather than challenged, institutional and formal power resulting in two joint male chairs.

As the status of domestic violence work shifts within the police, there has been a noticeable increased entry of men into DVUs. This has contradictory meanings and consequences. Whilst it confirms an increased commitment to domestic violence, it does so through a reinforcement of gender power, since 'importance' is defined in terms of a male presence. This is not to question either the ability of individual male officers or the importance of locating investigative officers within DVUs, but to point to the complexity of the issues involved. Not least being the actual or potential marginalisation of skilled and experienced women officers who built the foundations of different responses to domestic violence within the police service.

Issues of gender were also evident in some beat officers' responses to DVM. Both the DVM briefing sessions and the evaluation questionnaires prompted comments that the project was 'biased'. At issue here was the gender analysis of domestic violence which informed DVM's work. Despite the evidence of their own practice (that 90% plus of cases involve female victims – see Table 4.11) some officers continued to resist the implications of victims being disproportionately women and perpetrators correspondingly men. On the other hand there were officers who had a very clear awareness of the gender issues involved, and they expressed considerable frustration with the resistance of their colleagues to address these issues in their attitudes and practices. Sexual politics were always at play in this project, in obvious and not so obvious ways.

Interpersonal power

This form of power is impossible to distinguish in any clear way from the other forms detailed above. However, it is individuals who drew on these sources, or challenged them; and interpersonal dynamics, the taking up of positions, are one part of a complex equation. On one level oversimplifying these positions could be summarised as 'power seeking', 'power-mongering'; 'power-broking' and 'observing'. Each position (apart from observing, which may have been a chosen position or one required by the role of the individual, such as the evaluator and CPS representatives) could involve a range of behaviours, and be subject to various influences. These included but were not limited to: public discussions which involved attempts to persuade and/or explain a position; public posturing and overt power plays; private meetings and discussions; private and public interventions from, or entreaties to, hierarchies outside the locality and/or existing structures.

Individuals took up different positions and made differential contributions to the project over time. Some were more concerned with 'being there' contributing when there was something concrete they could offer, and observing the rest of the time. Others were preoccupied with 'being seen to be there', here connection to the project primarily served some other purpose. Some were primarily orientated to 'doing'; doing involved an explicit commitment to the project's aims, making available to DVM whatever skills and expertise they had to offer and, where appropriate and possible, attempting to create linked change within their own institutions. When power/glory seeking is at the fore for any individual they are either involved in explicit power machinations or supporting those of others to whom they owe allegiance. The 'doers' (or change makers) tend to prefer a power broking role, but may take up a position of power seeker/monger where prior agreements are reneged on.

The DVM staff also varied in how they used their interpersonal skills and knowledge over the lifetime of the project. In the first year there was a strong commitment within the staff team to establish DVM and make it work. This involved each of the workers finding a way to work with police officers, which was both approachable whilst retaining a critical perspective. Some of the staff team were able to use humour to good effect, others chose to meet with officers in informal settings. These strategies continued into the second and third years, but here more emphasis was placed on demonstrating the worth of DVM through professionalism in the work. The hostility DVM staff encountered from some officers may have resulted in a more defensive position, whereby the focus shifted to officers with whom good working relationships had already developed, or who showed an interest in the project and its work. Certainly by the middle of the final year the team was not using their individual and collective power to pull in the same direction.

Interpersonal power can be a positive resource, which benefits both the individual and the context they are working in; for this to be the case individuals must be working with an orientation which prioritises the overall 'best interests' of a project, rather than personal or even institutional interests. Within this framework must also be some acknowledgement that there may be genuine disagreements about precisely what the 'best interests' of a project might comprise. It is, however, only possible to honestly debate and explore such differences if there is a single agenda, as opposed to multiple, and frequently disguised, ones.

By way of a conclusion

Mark Liddle and Lorraine Gelsthorpe (1994) also provide a typology of forms of involvement which have a similarity with, although are more detailed than those outlined above. They identify six positions: prime movers; supportive passengers; sleeping partners; obstructors; agency 'spies'; and proselytisers. They also note three ways individuals and agencies orientate themselves to the task of the grouping, as gate keepers, gate openers or gate closers. All typologies are only useful if they are not seen as flat, static locations describing the totality of an agency or individuals' involvements. What they can do is highlight the positions taken at particular points in time, the consequences for the project, and how and why positions can change. For example, there has been more than one occasion in the history of DVM where a gate opener has become a gate keeper or closer and vice versa, where a prime mover became temporarily (either deliberately or through circumstance) a sleeping partner. These conceptual maps are not only relevant to how 'outsiders' (such as researchers) define positions, but also in exploring how insiders perceptions of each other affect working relationships and progress. For example, there is no doubt that some police officers viewed DVM as outsiders 'spying' on the police or 'proselytising' in relation to domestic violence, whilst others saw them as 'prime movers' in maintaining an impetus for change which they supported.

All inter-agency projects will comprise a variable combination of these orientations in the individuals involved. The particular combination will go some way to explaining the amount and extent of internal tension and external change which projects create. At several points in the history of DVM power issues took precedence, and this was always to the detriment of keeping track of, let alone achieving, DVM's aims. The overt power plays which dominated the first three months created a legacy of anxiety and unease which was never totally overcome.

There are many lessons to be learnt from DVM, some of which, not listed elsewhere, conclude this chapter. DVM would have benefitted from:

- A longer lead in time for the support workers would have enabled more skill sharing and more face to face contact with beat officers.

- Being located in one division; the two sites were always a compromise which at times meant that staff were juggling too many relationships and practices.

- A clearer sense from the outset of what skills were required from the support workers; the emphasis in initial recruitment was on skills and knowledge in relation to crisis intervention, but it rapidly became clear that organisational and administrative skills, as well as an ability to manage complex, and even conflictual, relationships were also core requirements.

- Consistent line management, and for small projects in large hierarchical organisations an advocate and problem solver.

- More emphasis on locating change makers within other agencies, especially those comprising the criminal justice system.

- A simplified management structure, so that where decision-making and accountability lay was transparent and action could be tracked relatively easily.

- A small (three or four members), but effective, implementation sub-group linked and reporting directly to the Management Committee.

7 Reflections, conclusions and recommendations

DVM was set up with three primary aims:

• to provide crisis intervention follow up to police responses to domestic violence calls;

• to develop stronger commitment locally to a law enforcement response;

• to encourage more consistent and co-ordinated responses amongst agencies in the borough, and identify gaps in provision.

The aims were extensive, and expecting all could be achieved effectively and concurrently within three years was unrealistic.

In making comparisons with the London, Ontario model it needs to be remembered that FCS had ten years to establish crisis intervention before enhancing law enforcement responses to domestic violence became a local priority. The emergence of their inter-agency model has been 20 years in the making. What might have been useful at the outset was a phased developmental plan, in which aspects were given chronological priority; this would have limited the sense of 'impossibility' which on occasion affected the staff team.

DVM's achievements and lessons learnt

The responses from women users of the service have, overwhelmingly supported the combination of police intervention and follow-up civilian support. There is also no question that the DVM model of crisis intervention has been effective, although not in the same ways for each individual. What matters is that most of DVM's users say the intervention made a difference, and the closer the intervention was to the model outline – personalised immediate contact soon after an incident – the more difference women report.

The irony for DVM staff, especially in the final year, was that the police did not make as extensive use of the service as they could have done. It became increasingly clear that without regular (at least once a month) reminders about DVM, officers who had not developed a routine of referring cases forgot about the project. This is a crucial lesson for any future 'replications'; that reminders about the service must be structured into police routines, rather than dependent upon project staff being able to attend training or briefing sessions.

Despite the under utilisation DVM worked intensively with more women than most other specialist domestic violence services are able to in any one year, as well as offering some level of support to a significant number of other women and to other agencies. The style of working represents a departure from previous responses; it does not wait for women to seek support, but is *pro-active*, engaging women initially and keeping in touch in order to accelerate change processes. DVM's model of crisis intervention has a great deal to offer both individuals and inter-agency working. It combines a one stop location for information and advice and co-ordination of responses with an interventionist pro-active response to recent incidents of violence. Users' evaluations demonstrate that for some women this speeds resolution, and produces more effective referrals; decreasing the 'revolving door' of distressed individuals being shunted between agencies, and decreasing the 'lottery' aspect of agency response, with chance and luck being replaced by more thoughtful and connected responses.

Australian research (Mugford, 1990) stressed the urgent need for 24-hour crisis intervention services in relation to domestic violence (including access for women whose first language is not English and women who use other forms of communication than speech). The level of 24-hour services in other western countries far exceeds that in Britain. DVM provided a locally based crisis intervention service, the only service of this kind currently in Britain.[39] It is however resource intensive, and the temptation to adapt the model – for example by using volunteers – will be strong. The complexity and potential dangers of crisis intervention should be borne in mind, as should cost effectiveness in terms of outcomes rather than simply expenditure. The savings in terms of police time, reduced repeat calls and appropriate referrals to other agencies are significant.

Enhancing law enforcement responses is more difficult to assess. Although there is some evidence to suggest slight movement in that direction in the recent arrest data, and examples of successful prosecutions, the limitations of the information available to us preclude any stronger statements, apart from the fact that the presence of DVM increased women's confidence in the

---

39 A single civilian worker, called the 'Women's Support Worker' has recently been employed by Central Scotland Police, funded by the regional Equal Opportunities Development Fund. Whilst charged with some of the same tasks as DVM, one individual working across an extensive geographic area, could not provide the same kind of crisis intervention as DVM.

police. What was indisputable was that the majority of victims calling the police want some form of action; action which protects her, action which constitutes an explicit challenge and sanction on abusive behaviour. Whilst police can only act within the law, there was substantial evidence that they were not always taking the law enforcement actions that they could have

There has not been the movement in relation to law enforcement which the project initially hoped for. Whilst some responsibility for that must lie with the local criminal justice agencies, other factors were also at play. The attitudinal barriers and routine trivialising of domestic violence, which the police surveys documented, suffuses the police service, despite policy changes, and was echoed in some of the attitudes and practices of prosecutors, magistrates and judges. Data from Greater Manchester (GMP, 1994, 1995) West Yorkshire (1993, 1994) and Northumbria (Walker and McNicol, 1994) echo Grace's (1995) findings: that arrest occurs in a minority of cases despite force policies promoting it (in Greater Manchester it was 13%, Northumbria 18%, and West Yorkshire 24%);[40] that in over a third of calls the perpetrator was not present when police arrived and minimal follow-up took place (Walker and McNicol report a 40% figure) despite circular 60/1990 prioritising "apprehension" of the offender; that there were inconsistencies between officers and forces in how cases are classified and recorded.

These continuing stumbling blocks have recently been added to by national changes in policing and criminal justice system practices (sectorisation, charging standards and case disposal), which are potentially in tension with circular 60/1990 and local domestic violence policies. By the third police questionnaire a significant minority of officers were citing these changes as factors which made arrest less likely and in interview some officers expressed strong opinions about the implications, both for domestic violence and policing more generally.

> *They say case disposal shouldn't have an influence on the decision you make at the scene – it shouldn't, but of course it does! You think 'I'm going to arrest this guy' and then you think 'case disposal'; you have to think of the work involved in an arrest, if you do it a number of times and they all come round 'no further action' that has an influence... I will freely admit that I will doctor it in order to get someone charged. I know I am wrong, but I think that case disposal is corrupt and immoral... A lot of my colleagues adhere to the system rigidly. Just because someone doesn't live on X estate doesn't mean they are any less guilty of a crime, or that they should not go before the court. But it's the ones from X estate that will go through. The goal is to ease the*

---

40   Some caution is needed in relation to the West Yorkshire figures since the number of incidents recorded were between a half and a third of those in the other areas. It is possible that only 'crimes' are being recorded, whereas in the other areas calls which are classified as 'no crimes' are also included.

load on the CPS, decrease the number of cases going to court. It's not about equity in prosecuting cases, it's money saving, cost cutting, nothing else.

Against this backdrop, and in this context, it is unrealistic to expect a small localised pilot with multiple aims to have significant impacts on policing and wider law enforcement practices.

Reflecting on what DVM could have done differently, some lessons for any future projects did emerge, which have not been highlighted already:

- A commitment from the outset to an agreed system of data collection and collation by the police, and regular updates being structured into project management meetings.

- A programmed series of training and feedbacks to beat officers which drew on what the project is learning and achieving.

A proportion of officers were interested in developing more consistent responses, they made the following suggestions; clear and 'strict' divisional guidelines which are not just advice, and more and better training which equipped officers to both understand and deal effectively with domestic violence.

In terms of inter-agency links and co-ordination some strong co-operative alliances developed and continue. It was, however, the day to day work of crisis intervention which had the most impact on the emergence of more co-ordinated and consistent responses. The level of suspicion and distrust which DVM encountered initially means that the respect they achieved locally by the end of the pilot was itself a significant achievement. To summarise:

- DVM achieved a significant amount in a relatively short period of time.

- Establishing and maintaining effective crisis intervention responses solely to victims of domestic violence in partnership with the police made DVM unique.

- There are no easy 'quick fixes' in either developing models of co-operative work between civilian staff and police or in developing law enforcement approaches to domestic violence by police and other criminal justice agencies.

Whilst DVM can undoubtedly claim meaningful achievements in relation to both crisis intervention and inter-agency co-ordination, the limitations in relation to law enforcement deserve more detailed discussion.

The domestic violence lottery

The pilot did tease out, in more detail than previously documented, some of the barriers to enhancing law enforcement responses. It also highlighted areas which require national, rather than local action if any substantial movement is to take place on these matters.

Within the police locally, whilst the overall support for a more positive response to domestic violence is to be noted and welcomed, the variability of understanding of, and responses to, domestic violence amongst them (by their own accounts and those of service users) highlight the need for increased input/training for police, which emphasises developing a common knowledge base and perspective whilst acknowledging the complexity of individual cases.

Police officers currently do not agree as to what counts as domestic violence, or what their role in response to it should be. This creates a lottery for victims, in which one officer will define her experience as violence, and respond to it as a crime, whilst another will not. Jalna Hanmer and Sheila Saunders' research in West Yorkshire confirms this inconsistent implementation of policy (see also for other British and international documentation, Fagan, 1996; Grace, 1995; Hilton, 1993; Jaffee et al. 1991; Walker and McNicol, 1994; Wright, 1995). Their survey demonstrated that police interventions were in line with the new policy in just over half of the cases, but in a significant number it replicated the traditional approach. Where perpetrators were present they were arrested in 40 per cent of cases, but in 25 per cent of cases police did not even talk to the abuser. Rebecca Morley and Audrey Mullender (1994) comment "not being present appeared to be the most effective means of avoiding police intervention" (p23). One of the mandatory arrest studies in the US included an 'offender-absent study'. Here in half of those cases where the assailant had left, an arrest warrant was issued. Interestingly this not only decreased the likelihood of further assaults for the group where warrants were issued, but it was more effective than arrest (Zorza, 1995). A coherent strategy is needed to address this issue (which this evaluation found occurring in a third of incidents); one possibility being that used by NIDVU of locating investigative officers within DVUs who have explicit responsibility for cases where perpetrators had left the scene.

Jeffrey Fagan (1996) argues that there are a range of factors which account for the difficulties bringing domestic violence into the criminal justice system: its epidemic proportions; its recurrence; that it usually takes place in private; and that the goals of the victim and the criminal justice system may not coincide. Kathleen Ferraro and Lucille Pope (1993) argue that there are irreconcilable differences between battered women, the police and the law. Whilst not agreeing with some of the conceptual distinctions made, the issues they raise need to inform the continuing debate in this area. They make the telling point that women's decision-making exists not in the arena of rational law, but in the complexity of relationships and connections with others; that compromises rather than decisions are reached, trade-offs in confusing and unpredictable contexts. Women who call the police wanting violence but not the relationship to end will seek different responses from women who want to or have already ended the relationship. The orientation of police officers, however, focuses on the here and now, the restoration of 'order' and 'peace'.

Women's needs reflect their current position on the continuum of adaption to violence. They simultaneously represent various levels of resources, concerns and knowledge of workable survival strategies. (Ferraro and Pope, p120)

Until police officers are able to not only understand this complexity, but also explore (rather than presume or infer) how women are using calling the police as a resource in their struggle to end violence, the perspectives of victims and police officers will, at times, be irreconcilable.

A number of other more general issues emerged as significant barriers to increasing, and making effective, law enforcement responses to domestic violence, which can only be addressed through national policy and legislation.

• Twenty years after the first call by government for accurate statistics on domestic violence calls to the police, there is still no nationally agreed format nor mechanism for their collection and collation. Establishing such processes (including making domestic violence a notifiable offence) should be a priority for the Home Office, since without them the commitment to responding to domestic violence as a crime cannot be meaningfully assessed.

• Police training needs to address the complexities of domestic violence including: the definition issue; coping strategies and how these are misinterpreted; what women want when they call the police; the complex decisions they have to make; the social, financial and emotional costs of domestic violence on individuals and agencies; and what increases both 'victim satisfaction' and women's safety.

- The increasing formal limitations on arrest make explorations of other approaches, such as the mandatory charging policy which exists in Ontario, a priority. Alternatively stronger moves towards a version of probable cause or mandatory arrest – one of which now pertains in every state in the US (Zorza, 1995)[41] – must be considered.

- Existing legislation cannot encompass the repeated ongoing nature of domestic violence, nor its particular forms and dynamics. Legislation should be considered which recognises it as a specific form of assault[42] (see also Smith, 1989), including: codifying and developing existing offenses (including, for example, stalking and harassment); supporting probable cause arrest; locating incidents with a context of repeat attacks; prioritising victim protection in sentencing policy. This would also address the definitional issues which currently undermine attempts to accurately estimate incidence and assess law enforcement responses.

- Experience in other jurisdictions suggests that developing the position, knowledge and expertise of special prosecutors positively affects prosecution rates. Within this the principle of direct contact between prosecutor and client, and/or victim witness support services are an essential component (see also Smith, 1989).

- The frequency with which injunctions, bail conditions and undertakings are breached, yet no further legal action is taken, seriously undermines women's right to protection under the law (as do the limits on availability of injunctions and the withdrawal of legal aid to obtain them), and compromises attempts to encourage and enable prosecutions. Urgent attention needs to be given to this area throughout the justice system.

Jane Ursel's (1996) recent review of reform over 15 years in the province of Manitoba, Canada illustrates the importance of visionary localised pilot projects which demonstrate the extent of change which new approaches can create – one example being the Winnipeg Family Violence Court increasing the willingness of police to arrest and pursue prosecution (p267). The existence of the court and a specialist prosecuting unit in turn resulted in swifter processing of cases, higher levels of successful prosecutions, primarily through guilty pleas. At the same time specialisation also enabled a redefinition of what counted as success; to explore the complexities of what women are seeking from criminal justice intervention. Similar lessons have been learnt from the DVM pilot.

---

41   This excellent review of the research, and report on findings of a survey by the National Center for Women and Family Law, notes that in several areas mandatory arrest was found to work best when combined with victim advocacy, such as that provided by DVM.

42   New Zealand now has an offence 'man assaults woman' to address this directly, and Peter Jaffee et al. (1993) point to the possibility of including a statutory responsibility on police to ensure women are protected if an arrest is not made.

DVM as a partnership project

All of the PDU projects involved forms of partnership, and the differing perspectives on what this entailed in relation to DVM were explored in Chapter Six. Mark Liddle and Lorraine Gelsthorpe produced a conceptual model of inter-agency and partnership approaches at the 1994 PDU spring seminar. As part of the conclusion to this report, I want explore to how far their insights apply to DVM. They note that in partnership projects:

> ... agencies... seldom share the same priorities, working practices, definitions of the problem, power or resource base... Inter-agency relations... are also highly complicated seldom static and influenced by a variety of institutional, individual and local/historical factors. (p2)

Each of these themes were relevant to DVM:

- DVM's priorities – achieving the aims of the project – had to compete with other priorities for the police, and some of the other agencies involved in the project. This lack of consensus can create tensions, and indeed did amongst a section of police resulting in some hostility towards not only the project, but the issue of domestic violence, even to the point where DVM were being held responsible for aspects of policing which were nothing more than implementation of police policy and existing legal statute.

- DVM worked in a different way to the police, and whilst this was understood as a complementary approach, there were occasions when different approaches and structures of decision-making came into conflict. It is to the credit of DVM that they stood their ground when issues of principle were involved. There were also examples of police officers learning from DVM, and adapting their approaches accordingly, alongside an increased awareness and understanding of the realities of police work amongst the DVM staff team.

- The issue of how domestic violence is defined, and what the appropriate response to it is underpins both differences of interpretation between DVM and the police, and between police officers themselves.

- Changes in personnel within the DVM staff team, both DVUs and police managers were a recurring feature throughout the pilot, requiring almost constant re-adjustment and under-cutting established relationships and routines.

Partnership projects, whilst currently encouraged and lauded, comprise both possibilities and tensions; in order to explore the potentials DVM had in the process to manage many and varied conflicting demands, priorities and tensions. If projects move beyond a surface linkage, then institutional and interpersonal dynamics are inescapable, involving issues of 'turf', perspective and power. Addressing and negotiating these created dilemmas for DVM.

On a broader level two recently published reflections on British responses to domestic violence (Hague and Mallos, 1993; Morley and Mullender 1994) expressed concern about the partnership between the police and DVM. The core issue at stake was whether this connection would compromise the project's independence and first line of accountability to victims. DVM has managed this tension in order to provide a different kind of intervention. One of the support workers concluded:

> *Funnily enough I think it is really important that we stay in the police station. Women call the police, we are giving the police credibility by our work and we get the chance to get out there, make contact fast. In terms of crisis intervention it wouldn't work if you were outside, a voluntary sector type organisation.* (SW4)

Accountability to women requires that we take their assessments of the service seriously, and the last words in this report are theirs. These are a (very) small selection from the many detailed responses women gave to an open ended question about locating a civilian crisis intervention team within a police station; they include younger and older women, black and white women, women who are and are not living with their partners, and women who did and did not pursue prosecution.

> *You're all great, there should be more people like you. I cannot fault you on one thing. Just thank-you for being there.*

> *I think there should be more of this with the police so as people can come to them without feeling that they are just another case of wasting police time. I got to know about you from a friend... some people bottle out from ringing the police.*

> *I am sure that every woman feels the same as me, but I feel that having a person not in uniform makes you feel more at ease and you don't feel so intimidated.*

> *I think the police do a very good job and I have the greatest respect for them. But I must say about the DVM, only for them there would be a lot of people that would not be here today. Only for them – I can't put*

into words how I feel about the DVM people, they are worth their weight in gold.

I think that DVM is a brilliant idea and although at the time I felt hassled by phone calls and letters as all I wanted was to be left alone, it really helped me not to brush the incident under the carpet, but admit to myself that it was serious and that I could prosecute my abuser if I wanted.

This is excellent, I can't say enough praise for the police and the DVM. They worked brilliantly together. The support was invaluable. Thank God for this place.

*I found the DVM support worker very helpful, the right person at the right time. I didn't know this was only available in Islington so feel lucky that I had the support and think it should be available to every woman who has been abused wherever she lives. The support I received in the early hours of the morning just after the incident saved me from cracking up. The phone call the next day convinced me that people **do** care and that I didn't have to face things alone.*

There should be more DVM units round the country with many more workers. This I am sure will be cost effective in the long run... The support I had was very, very good. Only a few phone calls to the DVM made a great difference to me.

I can say no more than thank you very much. The action I took I know was necessary, but I would never have made it on my own. My family would have convinced me to change my mind or I would have let it blow over if I had not had the chance to discuss it so openly.

Thanks to them I feel I have some control and have help available when I need without any pressure... I do think more women would come forward if they knew of DVM, and in time domestic violence would be taken seriously by society.

I think that it is good to have more time to focus and direct their attention to Domestic Violence Matters. Their input is much appreciated by the victims because the issue is dealt with as separate whereas the police see it as 'just another crime'. I would just like to take the opportunity to thank you Domestic Violence Matters for all your help and support over such an emotionally shattering experience. Your work will be appreciated and respected by many. I hope in the future that domestic violence will become more intolerable and unacceptable, not only for the victims but also for society as a whole. I wish you every success in all you do for us. Thank you.

The DVM worker informed me of my rights and spent time talking to me and giving helpful advice. I found the help and attention DVM gave me invaluable and as a result I am more likely to call the police if I am subjected again to violence in my own home.

Some women don't want to involve the police. I didn't want to get the police involved and they didn't pressure me to do that. I did in the end but I chose to do that myself and got major support at that time too.

I'd like to thank everyone at DVM for all the help and encouragement they have given me so far. I hope that the service continues for as long as it is needed and that loads and loads of women in abusive relationships hear about it and use it. There should be one in every area, not just Islington, but I'm glad I live in Islington because I have benefitted a great deal. Thank you and good luck.

References

Barron, Jackie (1990) *Not Worth the Paper...?: The Effectiveness of Legal Protection for Women and Children Experiencing Domestic Violence,* Bristol, WAFE.

Daly, Martin and Wilson, Margo (1993) 'Spousal homicide risk and estrangement' *Violence and Victims,* 8:1, 3–60.

Dixon, Bill, Kimber, Jan and Stanko, Betsy (1993) 'Sector policing, public accountability, and use of police services' paper at the *British Criminology Conference,* Cardiff.

Dobash, Rebecca and Dobash, Russell (1992) *Women, Violence and Social Control,* London, Routledge.

Edelman, Jeff and Eisocovits, Zvi (1996) *The Future of Intervention with Battered Women and their Families,* Newbury Park, Sage.

Fagan, Jeffrey (1996) *The Criminalisation of Domestic Violence: Promises and Limits,* Washington DC, National Institute of Justice.

Ferraro, Kathleen and Pope, Lucille (1993) 'Irreconcilable differences: battered women, police and law' in Hilton, Zoe (ed) op cit, 96–126.

Ford, David and Regoli, Mary Jean (1993) 'The criminal prosecution of wife assaulters: process, problems and effects' in Hilton, Zoe (ed) op cit, 127–164.

Glass, Dee Dee (1995) *'All My Fault': Why Women Don't Leave,* London, Virago.

Grace, Sharon (1995) *Policing Domestic Violence in the 1990s,* Home Office Research Study No. 139, HMSO.

Greater Manchester Police Authority (1994) *Domestic Violence Statistics.*

Greater Manchester Police Authority (1995) *Domestic Violence Statistics.*

Gordon, Linda (1988) *Heroes in Their Own Lives*, New York, Viking.

Hague, Gill and Malos, Ellen (1993) *Domestic Violence: Action for Change*, Cheltenham, New Clarion Press.

Hanmer, Jalna and Saunders, Sheila (1990) 'Women, violence and crime prevention: a study of changes in police policy and practices in West Yorkshire', *Violence Abuse and Gender Relations Study Unit Research Paper 1*, Department of Social Studies, University of Bradford.

Heise, Lori (1994) *Violence Against Women: The Hidden Health Burden*, Washington DC, The World Bank.

Hilton, Zoe (ed) (1993) *Legal Responses to Wife Assault: Current Trends and Evaluation*, Newbury Park, Sage.

Home Affairs Select Committee (1993) *Domestic Violence, Vol 1 Report and Proceedings of the Committee*, London, HMSO.

Home Office (1990) Circular 60/90, HMSO.

Jaffee, Peter; Thompson, Judy (1979) *Family Consultant Service with the London Police Force: A Prescriptive Package*, London (Ontario), London Family Court Clinic.

Jaffee, Peter et al. (1984) 'Evaluating the impact of a specialized civilian Family Crisis Unit within a police force on the resolution of family conflicts' *Journal of Preventative Psychiatry*, 2:1, 63-73.

Jaffee, Peter (1986) 'The impact of police charges in incidents of wife abuse' *Journal of Family Violence*, 1:1, 37-49.

Jaffee, Peter et al. (1991) *Wife Assault as a Crime: The Perspectives of Victims and Police Officers on a Charging Policy in London, Ontario from 1980-1990*, London (Ontario), Family Court Clinic Inc.

Jaffee, Peter et al. (1993) 'The impact of police laying charges' in Hilton, Zoe (op cit), 62-95.

Kelly, Liz (1995) 'Changing the law - the front and the back door' *Trouble and Strife*, 32.

Kelly, Liz (1996) 'Battered Women's Syndrome: Help or hindrance?' in *Justice for Women Information Pack* (second edition), London, Justice for Women.

Kelly, Liz (1997) Final report of activities of the EG-S-VL including Plan of Action for combating violence against women. Strasbourg, Council of Europe.

Kelly, Liz; Burton, Sheila and Regan, Linda (1996) 'Beyond victim and survivor: sexual violence, identity and feminist theory and practice' in Lisa Adkins and Vicki Merchant (eds) *Sexualizing the Social: Power and the Organisation of Society*, London, Macmillan.

Kelly, Liz; Burton, Sheila and Regan, Linda (1995) 'The dangers of using syndromes and disorders in legal cases' *Rights of Women Bulletin*, Spring.

Liddle, Mark and Gelsthorpe, Lorraine (1994) *Crime Prevention and Inter-Agency Co-operation*, Home Office Police Research Group, Crime Prevention Unit Series, Paper 53.

McGibbon, Alison; Cooper, Libby and Kelly, Liz (1989) *"What Support?": An Exploratory Study of Council Policy and Practice, and Local Support Services in the Area of Domestic Violence within Hammersmith and Fulham*, London, Hammersmith and Fulham Community Safety Unit.

McWilliams, Monica and Spence, Lynda (1995) *Criminal Justice System and Domestic Violence in Northern Ireland*, Centre for Research on Women, University of Ulster.

Mooney, Jayne (1994) *The Hidden Figure: Domestic Violence in North London, London*, Islington's Police and Crime Prevention Unit.

Morley, Rebecca and Mullender, Audrey (1994) *Preventing Domestic Violence to Women*, Home Office Police Research Group, Crime Prevention Unit Series, Paper 48.

Mugford, J (1990) 'Domestic violence in Australia: policies, practices and politics' *Australian Institute of Criminology*, Canberra.

Platform for Action, Report of the Fourth World Conference on Women, Beijing 4–15 September 1995. (United Nations publication, E96.IV.13).

Pleck, Elizabeth (1987) *Domestic Tyranny: The Making of Social Policy Against Family Violence from Colonial Times to the Present*, Oxford, Oxford University Press.

Smith, Lorna (1989) *Domestic Violence: An Overview of the Literature*, Home Office Research Studies No. 107, London, HMSO.

Ursel, Jane (no date) *Final Report: Year 1, Family Violence Court Winnipeg*, Department of Sociology, University of Manitoba.

Ursel, Jane (1996) 'The possibilities of criminal justice intervention in domestic violence: a Canadian case study' *Current Issues in Criminal Justice*, 8:3, 263-274.

Victim Support (1996) *Women, Rape and the Criminal Justice System*, London, Victim Support.

Walker, Janet and McNicol, Laura (1994) *Policing Domestic Violence: Protection, Prevention or Prudence*, Newcastle, Relate Centre for Family Studies.

West Yorkshire Police (1993) *Domestic Violence Survey*.

West Yorkshire Police (1994) *Domestic Violence Survey*.

Working Party on the Legal and Judicial Process (1996) *Victims of Sexual and Other Crimes of Violence Against Women and Children*, Dublin, The National Women's Council of Ireland.

Wright, Samantha (1995) *The Legal and Economic Dynamics of Domestic Violence*, PhD thesis, Nottingham Trent University.

Zorza, Joan (1995) 'Mandatory arrest for domestic violence: why it may prove the best first step in curbing repeat abuse' *Criminal Justice*, Fall, 2-9, 51-54.

Publications

List of research publications

The most recent research reports published are listed below. A **full** list of publications is available on request from the Research, Development and Statistics Directorate, Information and Publications Group.

Home Office Research Studies (HORS)

184. **Remand decisions and offending on bail: evaluation of the Bail Process Project.** Patricia M Morgan and Paul F Henderson. 1998.

185. **Entry into the criminal justice system: a survey of police arrests and their outcomes.** Coretta Phillips and David Brown with the assistance of Zoë James and Paul Goodrich. 1998

186. **The restricted hospital order: from court to the community.** Robert Street. 1998

187. **Reducing Offending: An assessment of research evidence on ways of dealing with offending behaviour.** Edited by Peter Goldblatt and Chris Lewis. 1998.

188. **Lay visiting to police stations.** Mollie Weatheritt and Carole Vieira. 1998

189. **Mandatory drug testing in prisons: The relationship between MDT and the level and nature of drug misuse.** Kimmett Edgar and Ian O'Donnell. 1998

190. **Trespass and protest: policing under the Criminal Justice and Public Order Act 1994.** Tom Bucke and Zoë James. 1998.

191. **Domestic Violence: Findings from a new British Crime Survey self-completion questionnaire.** Catriona Mirrlees-Black. 1999.

192. **Explaining reconviction following a community sentence: the role of social factors.** Chris May. 1999

Research Findings

63. **Neighbourhood watch co-ordinators.** Elizabeth Turner and Banos Alexandrou. 1997.

64. **Attitudes to punishment: findings from the 1996 British Crime Survey.** Michael Hough and Julian Roberts. 1998.

65. **The effects of video violence on young offenders.** Kevin Browne and Amanda Pennell. 1998.

66. **Electronic monitoring of curfew orders: the second year of the trials.** Ed Mortimer and Chris May. 1998.

67. **Public perceptions of drug-related crime in 1997.** Nigel Charles. 1998.

68. **Witness care in magistrates' courts and the youth court.** Joyce Plotnikoff and Richard Woolfson. 1998.

69. **Handling stolen goods and theft: a market reduction approach.** Mike Sutton. 1998.

70. **Drug testing arrestees.** Trevor Bennett. 1998.

71. **Prevention of plastic card fraud.** Michael Levi and Jim Handley. 1998.

72. **Offending on bail and police use of conditional bail.** David Brown. 1998.

73. **Voluntary after-care.** Mike Maguire, Peter Raynor, Maurice Vanstone and Jocelyn Kynch. 1998.

74. **Fast-tracking of persistent young offenders.** John Graham. 1998.

75. **Mandatory drug testing in prisons – an evaluation.** Kimmett Edgar and Ian O'Donnell. 1998.

76. **The prison population in 1997: a statistical review.** Philip White. 1998.

77. **Rural areas and crime: findings from the British crime survey.** Catriona Mirrlees-Black. 1998.

78. **A review of classification systems for sex offenders.** Dawn Fisher and George Mair. 1998.

79. **An evaluation of the prison sex offender treatment programme.** Anthony Beech et al. 1998.

80. **Age limits for babies in prison: some lessons from abroad.** Diane Caddle. 1998.

81. **Motor projects in England & Wales: an evaluation.** Darren Sugg. 1998

82. **HIV/Aids risk behaviour among adult male prisoners.** John Strange et al. 1998.

83. **Concern about crime: findings from the 1998 British Crime Survey.** Catriona Mirrlees-Black and Jonathan Allen. 1998.

84. **Transfers from prison to hospital - the operation of section 48 of the Mental Health Act 1983.** Ronnie Mackay and David Machin. 1998.

85. **Evolving crack cocaine careers.** Kevin Brain, Howard Parker and Tim Bottomley. 1998.

86. **Domestic Violence: Findings from the BCS self-completion questionnaire.** 1999. Catriona Mirrlees-Black and Carole Byron. 1999.

Occasional Papers

The impact of the national lottery on the horse-race betting levy. Simon Field and James Dunmore. 1997.

The cost of fires. A review of the information available. Donald Roy. 1997.

Monitoring and evaluation of WOLDS remand prison and comparisons with public-sector prisons, in particular HMP Woodhill. A Keith Bottomley, Adrian James, Emma Clare and Alison Liebling. 1997.

Evaluation of the 'One Stop Shop' and victim statement pilot projects. Carolyn Hoyle, Ed Cape, Rod Morgan and Andrew Sanders. 1998.

Requests for Publications

Home Office Research Studies, Research Findings and *Occasional Papers* can be requested from:

Research, Development and Statistics Directorate
Information and Publications Group
Room 201, Home Office
50 Queen Anne's Gate
London SW1H 9AT
Telephone: 0171-273 2084
Facsimile: 0171-222 0211
Internet: http://www.homeoffice.gov.uk/rds/index.htm
E-mail: rds.ho@gtnet.gov.uk